THE HEALING RIVER
and its contributing streams

Randy Clark

ENDORSEMENTS

"Randy has deeply impacted my life and our movement. He has been used to touch hundreds of thousands with God's healing love. His process and discovery of healing is sure to encourage you regardless of your background. Randy explains how God pours out His healing in greater measures in the midst of worshipping Him in the glory of His presence. When I read this, my spirit shouted "Yes and Amen!" May Randy's personal journey build faith to believe that God heals today. As you read The Healing River and Its Contributing Streams, I pray you receive an impartation to bring healing to the nations."

Dr. Heidi Baker, Ph.D.
Founding Director of Iris Global

I can think of no better person to write on the subject of healing and the church than Randy Clark. With his rich heritage, biblical truths and insights, personal experiences, and deep intimate relationship with God, Randy lays out a solid biblical foundation that healing is for today and you (the church) have been given authority to heal the sick. He discusses the various Christian healing streams, their impact on the church today, and dispels the myths and attitudes we have towards them to bring unity to the entire Body of Christ. This book is a must read.

Dr. Ché Ahn
Senior Pastor, HRock Church, Pasadena, CA
President, Harvest International Ministry
International Chancellor, Wagner Leadership Institute

As Jesus asked his disciples to heal the sick and proclaim the Kingdom of God (Luke 10:9), so does Randy Clark aspire to have the accord of diverse denominations through uplifting the various streams of healing within Christianity. Opposing the power of the enemy, Randy through this Spirit-filled book encourages the diverse denominations to build up "a greater love and respect" among them in working for healing together. It is time for the churches to hear Randy Clark's prophetic voice for the mighty flow of God's graceful river of healing and the cooperation of the churches for the sake of proclaiming God's Reign.

Dr. Andrew S. Park, Ph. D.
Professor of Theology and Ethics
United Teological Seminary, Dayton OH

ENDORSEMENTS

Randy Clark is not only at the forefront of an ongoing revival movement which has swept Christendom in recent history, but also an avid student of church history as he compellingly demonstrates in this book. He traces the streams and development of prominent healing movements throughout the development of Global Christianity—acknowledging their unique contributions or best practices, yet seeing them united under the ongoing "healing river" of the Holy Spirit. Randy does not merely draw from scholarly research to outline these streams, but also weaves in his own first-hand accounts of the miraculous and personal encounters with these different streams throughout his ministry. This book is definitely a must read. For the "healing river" of the Holy Spirit continues to flow to this day, it is high time that we rediscover the ministry of healing and restore its prominence in Christianity as Jesus intended it to be.

Dr. Luther J. Oconer, Ph.D.
Assistant Professor of United Methodist Studies
Director of the Center for Evangelical United Brethren Heritage
United Theological Seminary

In his new book, The Healing River, Randy Clark presents a history of the healing ministry from Biblical days to the present time. He has woven a rich tapestry that includes all churches and traditions culminating in the present day revival of healing in the Pentecostal and Charismatic renewal movements. Throughout, he weaves into the story his own personal experiences, including his part in the "Toronto Blessing" revival of the 1990's. A very interesting and popular history for laymen and clergy alike.

Dr. Vinson Synan, Ph. D.
Dean emeritus
Regent University

"Randy Clark has done the Church a great service is showing how healing was and is practiced in many parts of the Church. I resonate with Randy's desire to appropriate and appreciate the many methods and approaches used with good results in the various wings of the Church. Anyone who thinks healing is an obscure side issue will find this book a challenge to that idea. May all the streams of God come together in a mighty river of God's grace and power. Great job, Randy!"

Joe McIntyre
Author of E.W. Kenyon and His Message of Faith and Throne LifeFounder and Senior Minister Word of His Grace Church
and the Healing Centre www.wordofhisgracechurch.org
Empowering Grace Ministries
President, Kenyon's Gospel Publishing Society www.kenyons.org

the
HEALING
RIVER

and its contributing streams

RANDY CLARK

globalawakening

GLOBAL AWAKENING   1451 CLARK STREET   MECHANICSBURG PA   17055

THE HEALING RIVER AND ITS CONTRIBUTING STREAMS
by Randy Clark
© Copyright 2013 Randy Clark 1st Edition, March 2013 All rights reserved.

Edited by: Sue Thompson, Vicki West, and Bob Baynard

🐢globalawakening

Apostolic Network of Global Awakening
1451 Clark Street
Mechanicsburg, PA 17055

For more information on how to order this book or any of the other materials that Global Awakening offers, please contact the Global Awakening Bookstore.

ISBN: 978-0-9818454-1-8

Second Printing: February 2014.

Table *of* Contents

Acknowledgement

"I want to thank Sue Thompson for editing this book and helping to take once again various teachings from various sources to bring them together for this book. She took my vision and made it happen. I also thank Vicki West, one of my personal assistants who has helped me get my life back, by relieving the load of refining my documents for books and seminary. Thanks to Bob Baynard for his helpful suggestions, and once again heading up the publishing process once the final edit was available to him. Thank you Sue, Vicki, and Bob."

the healing river

Foreword

In The Healing River, Randy Clark has grasped a vital key to under-standing the weakness of the Church today in the face of the rise of other religions: "The New Age Movement would not have so large a following if the Church was moving in its divine right to heal and experiencing its divine empowerment made possible in the Holy Spirit. . . . The counter-feit is filling the void created by a form of Christianity that is less than it ought to be." A powerless church will be supplanted by false religions that demonstrate real, though ultimately malevolent, power.

Randy describes his own journey out of cessationism and his deep dive into God's river of healing. He explains the fascinating contradic-tion in his Baptist background that claimed the supernatural gifts of the Spirit such as prophecy, word of knowledge, and word of wisdom do not exist today, yet those same people were operating in the gifts, just calling them something else and not recognizing their supernatural nature. He has traced the various streams throughout church history where heal-ing has flowed, examining where the river has become stopped up, and suggesting how the Church can release the healing river once again.

Armin Gesswein, an evangelist with The Christian and Missionary Alliance, warned early in the 20th century of dispensationalizing away the power of the Holy Spirit: "Those who taught us the combination key [of dispensationalism] say, 'God doesn't do those things now. God doesn't work like that any more.' . . . Dispensationalism does not open the book of Acts and the power of God; it closes them. . . . it is arbitrarily super-imposed by man. . . . Wherever dispensationalism gets in, it kills the deep spirit of prayer and revival." Randy Clark exposes the withering de-supernaturalization of dispensationalism, and opens up for us once again the book of Acts and the power of God.

Anemic beliefs in healing and anemic prayers for healing result in anemic healings. When I was diagnosed with cancer in 2007, I realized that anemic prayers of "If it be Thy will" were not going to be effective against a disease that kills. Power-packed, authoritative, faith-filled, expectant praying was essential to my healing. What Randy calls "soft cessationism" has given lip service to the power of God but has pre-vented expectation of God's power to work significantly today or even of God's desire to heal today. An over-emphasis on the sovereignty of God has failed to recognized the part of God's nature that He Himself has re-vealed to us is as a healer - "I am Yahweh Rapha" - the Lord our Healer (Exodus 15:26).

We don't see God's miraculous healing power because we don't expect it. We don't expect it, first, because we have not realized that it is God's nature to heal. Secondly, we don't expect it because we have not seen it, so we have to find a way to explain away the lack of miracu-lous power. We thus have a truncated theology of God's nature. Baptist pastor and theologian A.J. Gordon, founder of what is now known as Gordon-Conwell Seminary, understood this when he declared, "Faith for healing cannot rise above the general level of the Church's faith." Likewise, A.B. Simpson, the former Presbyterian who founded the Higher Life movement known as The Christian and Missionary Alliance, challenges us to have expectation for the supernatural: "The signs of healing do not follow all believers, but they follow those who believe for the signs."

Randy Clark in The Healing River has encouraged and challenged us, both from Scripture and testimony, to expect the supernatural power of God. He has written the heart of what Armin Gesswein proclaimed: "But how bracing in this day of need to know that we are still in the dis-pensation of the Holy Spirit just as in the Acts, and that God can baptize and fill believers with His Spirit, set churches on fire, and through them bring sinners to repentance and to Christ. . . . For neither the promise of the Holy Spirit nor the promised Holy Spirit has been withdrawn, except where men no longer want Him as the first Christians did."

Randy Clark inspires us to let all of the healing streams flow once again in God's great healing river. Let the river flow!

Dr. Paul L. King, D.Min., D.Th.

Doctor of Ministry Mentor, United Theological Seminary

Author of 10 books, including:

God's Healing Arsenal, Genuine Gold, and Come Up Higher

2006 Oral Roberts University Faculty Scholar of the Year

the healing river

Introduction

O ver a quarter of a century ago, while I was in college and then seminary, I read about a famous, highly educated Methodist minister named Dr. Leslie Weatherhead who had a large church called City Temple Congregational Church in London in the mid-20th century. In this church Dr. Weatherhead established a clinic for healing, bringing together ministers, psychologists, and medical doctors to work in tandem for the healing of people's illnesses. He wrote his doctoral dissertation at Oxford University on *Psychology, Religion, and Healing*, and that dissertation became a book. He then went on to put into practice his belief in God's power to heal. He predicted that what was to him a theory would one day be proven by medical science. He said, "that religion, which has, as one of its main functions, the altering of a person's emotions from negative to positive, from fear to trust, from hate to love, and so on, may be seen to be of supreme relevance in the prevention and healing of disease, including organic disease."[1] Today there is an established school of medicine that is based upon Dr. Weatherhead's theory which is now scientific fact. This special field of medicine, this school of medicine, is called the school of Psychoneuroimmunology.

Today I find more schools of medicine open to the power to heal through non-traditional medical means than I do divinity schools, and more gradates of medical schools (MDs) open to healing than graduates from seminaries (M.Div.s). No wonder there is so little real expectancy for receiving healing through prayer in many of the churches of America and Western Europe. Their pastors have been trained in unbelief regarding healing through prayer by the very seminaries established to train them for ministry.

There are two main sources for this unbelief, this lack of expectancy for divine healing through prayer. One is liberalism, based upon rationalism, which doesn't believe in anything supernatural happening today because of liberalism's belief in a world that is basically deist. In a deist worldview God would not violate his *laws of nature*. The other main source causing such terrible unbelief, this disempowering force regarding expectancy of a miracle, is Cessationism, which believes God did do miracles through Jesus and the apostles, but after the death of the apostles and their immediate successors, these gifts of healings and miracles died along with the offices of healer. (1 Corinthians 12:28ff.)

There are now, today, two things happening at the same time regarding healing. One is the New Age Movement with its strong emphasis upon healing. The other is the move of God within the Church, which is currently experiencing a powerful revival of healing and rediscovering the message of the Kingdom of God. This current move of God is more characteristic of the Church south of the equator where Christianity is growing most rapidly, and where most Christians live today, but it is also beginning to advance in North America, and in Europe, today's dark continents of unbelief.

What can we do to return to the kind of Christianity Jesus died to establish, and Paul died to strengthen? We must first realize that what much of the Church has been experiencing falls short of the experiences of the early Church for the first 300 years of Christianity. If we look at the Faith Cure Movement of the 19th century we see that they understood the deception of the enemy that found expression in Christian Science, New Thought, and Unity. These three arose shortly after the Church began to recover the healing ministry of Jesus, and would never have been able to get a foothold if the Church had been walking in the power of the Holy Spirit, especially in regard to healing. The same is true today as well. The New Age Movement would not have so large a following if the Church was moving in its divine right to heal and experiencing its divine empowerment made possible in the Holy Spirit.

We need to receive what Jesus died to give. The counterfeit is filling the void created by a form of Christianity that is less than it ought to be. We Christians need to rediscover again the emphasis, the importance, and the proper place of the ministry of healing within Christianity and within our personal lives as Christians.

More than any other of the major world religions, Christianity places the greatest emphasis upon healing. About one-fourth of the verses in the gospels deal with Jesus healing someone, or explaining healing, or going to heal someone, or commissioning his disciples to heal the sick. This emphasis on healing continues in the first recorded history of Christianity, the book of Acts. It is also evident in the epistles with mention of signs and wonders, which includes the ministry of healing as the primary display of a sign or wonder. Paul, near the end of his most doctrinal epistle says:

*For I would not dare say anything except what Christ has accomplished through me to make the Gentiles obedient by **word and deed**, by the **power of miraculous signs and wonders**, and by the **power of God's Spirit**. As a result, I have **fully** proclaimed the good news about the Messiah from Jerusalem all the way around to Illyricum.*

(Romans 15:18-19 emphasis mine. HCSB)

Again, in 1 Corinthians 4:20 Paul says, *"For the kingdom of God is not in word but in power."* (NASB)

The gospel of Jesus and his apostles was the gospel of the Kingdom of God. This Kingdom dawned with the coming of Jesus and is to be ever increasing. The "gates of hell" will not be able to stand the advance of the Church with its message of the Kingdom of God which is based upon the revelation that Jesus is the Christ. Like leaven, the Kingdom is to eventually leaven the whole lump, to affect all the systems of the world, just as the mustard seed continues to grow until it is the largest plant in the garden (Cf. Luke 13:18,21).

Jesus told his disciples that when someone experienced deliverance, the Kingdom of God had come upon them. *"If I drive out demons by the finger of God, then the kingdom of God has come to you."* (Luke 11:20 NIV) Jesus saw healing and deliverance as the two most important aspects of the Kingdom of God that had been inaugurated in His incarnation. Luke's gospel makes this powerfully clear.

Then He sent them to proclaim the kingdom of God and to heal the sick.
                                                          (Luke 9:2 NIV)

When the crowds found out, they followed Him. He welcomed them, spoke to them about the kingdom of God, and cured those who needed healing.
                                                          (Luke 9:11 HCSB)

Heal the sick who are there, and tell them, 'The kingdom of God has come near you.'   (Luke 10:9 HCSB)

Acts continues Luke's record of the importance of healing as part of the message of the Kingdom of God.

But when they believed Philip, as he preached the good news about the kingdom of God and the name of Jesus Christ, both men and women were baptized.
                                                          (Acts 8:12 HCSB)

Philip was an evangelist and believed by many to be one of the first deacons of the Church; however, he was not an apostle, thus proving that healing isn't just the domain of the apostles. In context, the revival Philip led in Samaria was accompanied by healings, deliverances, and demonstrations of the Spirit's presence.

As we examine together several of the healing streams that flow into God's mighty river, I want to show the value of each, seeing something good in each one. This approach will, hopefully, help to reduce the negative criticism by one stream about another. It is my great desire to promote unity among all the various streams of healing within Christianity. I long to see a greater love and respect develop among the various streams of healing today, reducing our judgments of one another and delivering us from our "mean spiritedness," even though this "mean spiritedness" can come from what some may think is a noble purpose - to purify the church of (what they believe is) incorrect doctrine.

It is my belief that much of the hostility and fighting between the various camps of Christian healing springs from the deception of the enemy who comes to steal the word of God, preventing us from bringing forth a harvest of 30, 60, and 100 fold (Matthew 4:20). The devil has never feared our desire to get from earth to heaven but he has great fear of us wanting to bring the power and authority of heaven to earth. The enemy of our souls works extremely hard to distract us from the reality of the good news that the Kingdom of God has come to this world in Jesus Christ. He would like to keep us focused on heaven and forgiveness in the hope that we do not notice the present reality of the availability of the power of the Kingdom here on earth. Through doctrinal strongholds he and his demonic philosophies have been used to try to stop the fulfillment of Jesus' prayer, "... *thy Kingdom come. Thy will be done, on earth as it is in heaven."* (Matthew 6:10)

I have confidence that God is going to cause a great revival to occur in this time of a great population explosion. He is not going to let this generation go into eternity with the majority of the souls having no hope of eternal life. I believe God is going to breathe upon His whole Church, including the Roman Catholic, and Orthodox, as well as the Historical Protestant and Free Church traditions, awakening them to His power not only to save, but also to heal and deliver. He is not going to let this generation, in which more souls are facing eternity than any time since the beginning of mankind, slip into eternity without hearing the message of the "Kingdom of God" which is the good news that God has broken into our existence, has come near to reconcile, forgive, regenerate, and adopt.

His main calling card, God's main plan of evangelism is to demonstrate His power through healing and deliverance. The power to heal and deliver is not given to prove the truth of the message primarily,[2] but to demonstrate the message of a compassionate God who cares about our lives here as well as in the hereafter. The power to heal and to deliver is part of the gospel and as such should accompany the proclamation of the gospel. Healing and deliverance pertain to the gospel and are included in it. The coming of Heaven/Jesus with the power of the Kingdom of God has been made available to His followers who have entered the Kingdom in the present and are waiting for the consummation of that same Kingdom. Until that time we will continue to experience both the "Kingdom Now and Not Yet." We will see advances of the Kingdom of God, but also places where the Kingdom contracts as it did when the Muslims almost destroyed the Church in Central Asia and the Middle East. We will experience wonderful healings – thrills of victory, and also agonies of defeat when the loved ones we are praying for are not healed. It is in these times that we live in the mystery of God's ways and the conflict of two kingdoms.

endnotes

1 Leslie Weatherhead, *Psychology, Religion and Healing.* (New York, NY: Abingdon-Cokesbury Press. Stewart Press, 2007), 367-368.

2 Jon Ruthven, *On the Cessation of the Charismata: The Protestant Polemic on Post-Biblical Miracles,* Revised and Expanded Edition. (Tulsa, OK: Word and Spirit Press, 1993, 2011).

the healing river

PART ONE

Personal Journey –
Discovering the Gospel of the Kingdom

the healing river

CHAPTER ONE

Personal Journey from Cessationist Fundamentalism, through Skeptical Liberalism, to Expectation for Healing and Miracles Today

---

I have experienced or been part of almost all of the healing streams that we are going to examine. My story begins in the Baptist denominations; the General Baptist, Southern Baptist, and American Baptist. I have always believed in healing. I can't recall a time when I did not. Growing up I remember watching Oral Roberts' big tent healing crusades on television. I remember my maternal grandmother's story of healing well, even though I was only five years old when she shared with me how God miraculously and instantly healed her of a large goiter in her throat. I remember praying together as a congregation for the sick, but only a few times. Healing prayer in church was not normative in the churches of my childhood because they embraced a form of what we now call "soft cessationism."

Soft cessationist belief holds that the gifts of healing no longer exist in the Church today; that the office of healer no longer exists, and that tongues, prophecy, words of knowledge, and miracles have all ended. The pastors, churches and congregations of my childhood believed that God could heal, and that the Holy Spirit could, in His sovereignty, move in answer to prayer and heal those we prayed for, but there were no healing services. If you had introduced a healing segment into the order of the service with any regularity you would have had with the Baptist

Association or the Presbytery of the General Baptists.

Interestingly enough, within the small General Baptist church I grew up in, several people moved in prophecy and words of knowledge but did not realize they were operating in these gifts. While they were busy denying the charismatic or Pentecostal terms for these gifts they were actually functioning in them. They would communicate their impressions or knowings using language such as, "God told me," or "the Lord was showing me" or "I believe the Lord was leading me."

The pastors of the churches I grew up in were not well educated. None had degrees from seminary or college and most did not have a high school education. I would be sixteen years old before I would hear a college educated pastor, Brother Billy Duncan. Brother Duncan was a spiritual man who had had an encounter with God that made him different from most of the other pastors in the association. Although mostly untrained, these pastors had been influenced by soft cessationism. They believed God could heal as the sovereign Lord, and that He might answer our prayers if it was His will. Although they believed in healing to the extent they prayed for the sick, there was not strong faith for healing.

The Effect upon the Pastors and Worship Service

Within this theology of healing there was no place for healing in the normal order of service. Pastors did not feel any need to learn how to cooperate with the Holy Spirit or to move in the gifts of the Spirit as they pertained to healing. Healing was possible but not normative. In addition, we did not see very many of the people we prayed for healed, and we did not understand why. We believed the lack of healing was connected to the will of God, God's sovereignty, and God did not seem to be very willing to heal.

Only rarely were there special times of prayer for healing when someone was present to receive the prayer. During these times the person came to the front of the church and usually knelt down at a small altar in front of the pulpit. Then the pastor with the deacons would come and kneel beside the person to offer prayer for healing. Sometimes the person was anointed with oil, but not very often (this was seen to be more of a Pentecostal act). After the pastor and deacons had come to surround the person in prayer many others from the church would leave their pews to go kneel behind this group. Those closest to the sick person put their hands on their head, back, and shoulders. Then as the pastor began to pray the deacons would join in simultaneously and so would the rest of the people. Those who couldn't touch the sick person touched the person in front of them who was touching the person in front of them so that they were all linked together. Usually their prayer ended in "If it be thy will" and "asking in "Jesus' name." The fruit of these rare occasions of prayer for someone for healing in the service were mixed. A few were healed but most were not.

There was no teaching or preaching series on healing or a theology of healing, and rarely any sermons dealing with healing. Even if a text contained a healing it was spiritualized to make a moral or spiritual ap-plication rather than as a model for how to pray for the sick for physical healing.

During these growing up years my perspective on healing began to undergo change. Although I knew about my grandmother's healing, and at the age of twelve saw my Sunday school teacher healed, I watched my beloved grandfather die a terribly painful death from cancer despite much prayer on his behalf. By the age of sixteen I was confused about healing and couldn't reconcile the two sides of healing as I had seen them play out in the lives of my family and my church. I had no idea that two years later my perspective on healing would undergo radical trans-formation.

At the age of eighteen, I almost died in a car accident. It was a mir-acle I survived. I had multiple injuries to my face which required sixty stitches. There were fractures of the bones in my face, especially on my forehead which had three places the size of quarters that were crushed, my jaw was broken. I had ten to twenty percent compression of the verte-brae in my mid spine, paralysis of my digestive system, and other serious injuries. Three specialists converged on me and began to use the best medical science could offer to put my broken body back together. Due to the severity of my back injuries there was a possibility I would suffer permanent paralysis. They told me I would be hospitalized for forty-nine to seventy-seven days. I did not know how serious my injuries were, but once I regained consciousness I started telling everyone that I was going to the special evangelism meetings to be held at my church in less than a month.

In the days following the accident I was visited by my Baptist pastor who prayed for me, as well as my great uncle, a Pentecostal minister, and family and friends who prayed for my healing. Injuries that should have required surgery and taken months to heal were healed in a matter of weeks without surgery. To everyone's amazement I was completely healed and released from the hospital in twenty days, in time to give testimony of my healing at our church just like I said I would. About eight months later I was back working in the oil fields, a very laborious job with much lifting, completely healed. I had been told not to lift over ten pounds for a year, and some of the wrenches in the oil fields weighed more than ten pounds each.

This experience dramatically changed my personal view of healing. Within three months I had switched colleges and abandoned the pursuit of a teaching degree to enroll in a Christian college with a major in religious studies. I had no idea that my time in college and seminary would present another challenge to my views on healing and create in me a crisis of faith for a time.

From January 1974 through December 1977 I trained for ministry, first at a General Baptist College, today known as Oakland City University, and then at The Southern Baptist Theological Seminary. Almost all of my professors were liberal in their teaching. By liberal I mean they embraced a view that God doesn't break into our world in response to prayer in a way that would violate the "laws of nature" which He has established. Not only was there little expectation of miracles for today; some professors believed the miracles in the Bible were legendary or mythological.

This was indeed a crisis of faith for me which challenged my views of healing to the extent it almost destroyed my Christian faith. At one point I stopped believing in demons and angels and natural miracles, even those recorded in the Bible. The one anchor during this time, the one thing that kept me from losing my faith, was that I never doubted for a moment that God had healed me. My miraculous healing was very real and was a contradiction of the liberalism that pervaded my education.

Because of my own experiences in seminary, I believe that the majority of seminary trained ministers within the mainline denominations of today have little faith for anything supernatural to happen. I believe many do not believe in healing today even to the point of doubting it in biblical texts, so influenced are they by the liberal teaching they received in college and seminary based on the "higher-critical method" of studying the Bible. I believe most people setting in the pews would be shocked if they knew how skeptical the pastor standing behind the pulpit really was in regard to the supernatural, skeptical even regarding the biblical instances of healings and miracles.

While in seminary I wrote a paper for a New Testament class titled *The Historical-Critical Method: Interpreting the Bible and the Miraculous*. This paper resulted in a long discussion with the professor who at one point told me, "Healing is not central to the gospel, it is only peripheral." I felt strongly that he was wrong. He also told me that my commitment to healing would get me in trouble within the Baptist denomination. He was right about that.

Although this paper was written in 1976, I think the ideas put forth are still pertinent to our current discussion of the streams that make up the healing river of God, so I have included two references from the paper here. It is the early thinking of a twenty-four year old student in seminary. This paper really caused me to rethink what I believed about the supernatural. This was the seed that has since matured.

The Historical-Critical Method: Interpreting the Bible and the Miraculous. Studying religion at college and later, studying at a Baptist seminary, I was taught that the proper method of interpreting the Bible was to use the historical-critical method. This method involves studying the historical setting, studying the meaning of the original languages (Greek and Hebrew), and studying the source critics, form critics, text critics, etc. However, one of the unspoken presuppositions of this method is its naturalistic, philosophical bias. The supernatural is not accepted because the method's presuppositions are based upon Aquinas' synthesis of Aristotelian philosophy (which had no room for the supernatural) and the Christian faith. Walter Wink states in his book, *The Bible In Human Transformation: Toward a New Paradigm for Biblical Study*, "Historical biblical criticism is bankrupt." He further states, "The historical critical method had a vested interest in undermining the Bible's authority, that it operated as a background ideology for the demystification of religious tradition, that it required functional atheism for its practice, and that its attempted mastery of the object was operationally analogous to the myth of Satan and the legend of Faust. It was Van Harvey in his book, *The Historian and The Believer: The Morality of Historical Knowledge And Christian Belief*, who first made me aware of the logical consequence of applying the historical method completely to the biblical text. The result would be the denial of anything supernatural including the incarnation and the resurrection. Dr. Frank Tupper, (my former professor at The Southern Baptist Theological Seminary), in a lecture during the course on "Biblical Authority and the Modern Mind", expressed faith in the resurrection as a historical fact. However, he tended to see the miracles as mythological and legendary. It is apparent that Dr. Tupper here is following Dr. Pannenberg of South Africa. I do not see how one can accept the resurrection and deny the miraculous. Dr. Tupper, in his lectures, stated, "The unusual event of the resurrection will be analogous to the experience of all in the consummation." However, healing will also be analogous to all our experiences at that time.[2] (By consummation I am referring to the second coming of Jesus.)

And, from near the conclusion of the term paper:

The incarnation is the miracle of miracles. If our world system is open so that the incarnation can occur then it is open for miracles to occur." Dr. Polhill had stated in his lectures on *The Miracle Stories in the Gospels*, that his problem in regard to miracles deals with the incarnation. How can Jesus be fully man and have the power to perform miracles? How could modern man identify with that kind of Jesus?" At that time I tried to resolve the problem by pointing to the dual nature of Jesus and quoting the orthodox position of the Council of Nicaea 325 A. D. that Jesus was "very man of very man and very God of very God, without being a tertian quid." I now realize that the answer is that Jesus did miracles by the power of the Holy Spirit. That same power is available to all believers today. Jesus was not able to do anything of his own accord (John 5:19, 30; 8:28). Only what he saw the Father doing could He do (John 5:19). Before his baptism in power at the river Jordan, He performed no miracles (Luke 5:17b). He did his mighty deeds through the anointing power of the Holy Spirit. This view is based upon the Kenotic passage of Philippians 2, and is very important for our understanding of Jesus as our model for ministry. He was dependent upon the Holy Spirit. Jesus has given the Holy Spirit to us to enable us to fulfill the Great Commission of Matthew 28:19-20.

The In-break of the Kingdom of God and Miracles: If in the life and ministry of Jesus the in-break of the Kingdom of God occurred, then it seems natural that there would be conflict between Jesus and the evil forces in man and nature. It was because a conflict actually did occur and Jesus was victorious, that the early church attributed Lordship to him. If these conflicts had not occurred I would be most skeptical of the idea that in Jesus the in-break of the Kingdom occurred. Without the miraculous, Jesus would be another ideal moral prophet like Gandhi of India, or Buddha, and nothing more to me. He would be only one of the great religious leaders of the world. The miraculous element in Christianity and the belief that God can act in this world of ours is essential to the vitality of Christianity. Without this aspect, prayer becomes meaningless. One should study the social sciences rather than the Bible, and Theology should be replaced with Anthropology. Preaching which is void of the above concepts is one reason for the phenomenal growth of the Charismatic Movement, a movement reacting to the dead orthodoxy of much of Christianity. Just as Jeremiah criticized the Jews for creating with their hands gods who were helpless, modern man has created a "god" who is helpless to act in this world, a "god" to whom I refuse to bow down and worship.[3]

Today, I would change the above paragraph that was written in 1976 from the phenomenal growth of the Charismatic Movement to the phenomenal spread of the New Age Movement also caused by the dead orthodoxy of much of Christianity. I do not want the reader to think there are similarities between the New Age movement and the Charismatic movement or draw a negative conclusion from this statement. I, in fact, believe the answer to the advance of the New Age movement is the Pentecostal and the Charismatic movement.

There are actually many parallels between the New Age movement and Christianity, but the parallels do not have the same causative power behind them, and the source of revelation for each is very different; so different, in fact, that the causes and the resultant beliefs of the two are mutually exclusive. The New Age recognizes this and many of its key leaders are violently opposed to Christianity. *(See Christianity and Scientific Reductionism as the Two Main Obstacles to the Dawning of the "Age of Aquarius."* Also, see my book *Healing Energy: Whose Energy Is It?*[4]) A generation has arisen that is hungry for the reality of God's presence and who will no longer be satisfied with propositional truths about God; they want to experience God.

Interestingly enough, the liberal and the fundamentalist have become strange bed-fellows when it comes to healing. Liberalism, and fundamentalism, which is Cessationist in its understanding of healing, end up at the same place. Neither the pastors trained in a liberal seminary, nor the pastors trained in a fundamentalist Bible school typically have healing services in their churches. They do not try to learn how to flow in the gifts of the Spirit, and they do not feel a need to equip the saints for the work of healing ministry because they do not believe in it.

The liberal pastor believes God never violates the laws of nature. The fundamentalist pastor who believes the Bible is the inerrant word of God in all aspects of life, and believes that miracles and healings are historical events, doesn't believe healing happens today because the gifts of healing ended with the death of the Apostles, and miracles were given to establish the truth of the gospel and the Church. Once the church and its doctrines were established, the gifts of healing had served their purpose and were not to be expected any longer.[5] In this way the liberal pastor and the fundamentalist pastor become strange bedfellows, neither of whom equips their parishioners for healing or deliverance, though for very different theological reasons. Yet the practical outcome for the parishioners is the same - they are not taught to expect healing or how to pray for healing.

Upon graduation from seminary in 1977, I went to the American Baptist Church in Spillertown, Illinois where I pastored until 1984. I pastored for a total of fourteen years, mostly in the American Baptist denomination. During those fourteen years I learned a lot. I came to a better understanding of the struggles people and families go through, and I was privileged to get to know some wonderful people. I learned the importance of respect for the office of pastor, especially when I came to the end of myself; my abilities, my education, and "my" ministry. I had stood by many a hospital bed during those fourteen years, and conducted many funerals for my parishioners and their loved ones, including infants and children. I had prayed for some to be healed, but had seen little healing.

It was at this low point that I felt God speak to me to do three things. First, I was to preach differently; no more three points and a poem. I was to teach on larger passages from the gospels, emphasizing the words and works of Jesus - his message and ministry. Second, I was to teach that

God still heals today. Third, I was to have a conference at my church on healing. These impressions were so strong that I was quite shaken and wept from the visitation. I was convicted that things had to change.

Led by the Holy Spirit I invited a man named Blaine Cook to my church to teach on healing prayer. I had never met Blaine but I knew he was one of the most anointed leaders in the Vineyard Movement. I sent out invitations to all of the American Baptist pastors in the Midwest, and all the Evangelical pastors in southern Illinois, but I purposely did not invite the Pentecostals or the Charismatics because I did not want the Evangelical pastors to be scared off by the greater freedom of expression of Pentecostals and Charismatics. A portion of the invitation read, "If you have felt like there has to be more power for healing than what you are experiencing, and are tired of going to the hospital and praying, 'God guide the surgeon's hand,' and, if you want to learn how to pray more effectively for physical healing, then come to this seminar."

They came, in droves. The church was filled with pastors and leaders as well as members of my own church. Then God showed up! I had never seen power like this before in my life. Many were filled with the Holy Spirit. Five months later I felt led of the Spirit to leave the Baptist denomination, to fulfill the call that had been placed on my heart at the age of eighteen - to plant a church. I still thank God for everything that happened to me as a result of that first meeting on healing prayer. He messed up my comfortable life in order to prepare me to step out of my comfort zone and follow Him into the River of Healing.[6]

endnotes

[1] Van A. Harvey, *The Historian and the Believer: The Morality of Historical Knowledge and Christian Belief* (New York, New York: The MacMillan Company, 1966, 1996).

[2] Randy Clark, *The Relation of the Problem of Miracle to the New Testament Interpretation and Christian Faith,* A Paper Submitted to Dr. John Polhill of the Department of New Testament Interpretation Southern Baptist Theological Seminary in partial fulfillment for the requirement for Course N.T. S 33H "A study on the book of Acts" (Louisville, KY, January 28, 1977), 24.v

[3] Randy Clark, *The Relation of the Problem of Miracle to the New Testament Interpretation and Christian Faith,* A Paper Submitted to Dr. John Polhill of the Department of New Testament Interpretation Southern Baptist Theological Seminary in partial fulfillment for the requirement for Course N.T. S 33H "A study on the book of Acts" (Louisville, KY, January 28, 1977), 25.

[4] I have a power point with over 50 slides that are quotes revealing how antagonistic towards Christianity and science are key New Age leaders, or those whose thought is heavily drawn upon within the New Age. The references are from: Wouter J. Hanegraaff, *New Age Religion and Western Culture: Esotericism in the Mirror of Secular Thought* (Albany, New York: State University of New York Press, 1988). The slide presentation is available from the online bookstore at Global Awakening.com At the bookstore type into the search window, "Quotes from Wouter Hanegraaff PowerPoint." This will take you to the downloadable power points where they may be purchased. This is by far the most scholarly work I have seen on understanding the beliefs of New Age and the movements and philosophies of the 19th and 20th centuries that have fed it and helped it develop.

[5] See the following works to understand why the teachings of cessationism and liberalism are inadequate to faithful obedience to the Lord and the Bible. Jon Ruthven, *On the Cessation of the Charismata: The Protestant Polemic on Post-Biblical Miracles,* Revised and Expanded Edition (Tulsa, OK: Word and Spirit Press, 1993, 2011). Jon Ruthven, "Correction on Apostolic Writings" (November 16, 2010). Jon Ruthven, *What's Wrong With Protestant Theology?: Traditional Religion vs. Biblical Emphasis* (Tulsa, OK: Word and Spirit Press, 2013). Jon Ruthven, *The Prophecy That Is Changing History: New Research on Ezekiel's Vision of the End* (Fairfax, VA: Xulon Press, 2003). Gary Greig, *The Kingdom and the Power: Are Healing and The Spiritual Gifts Used By Jesus and the Early Church Meant For the Church Today?,* ed. Gary Greig and Kevin Springer (Ventura, Ca: Regal Books, 1993). Gary Greig, "The Purpose of Signs and Wonders in the New Testament: What Terms for Miraculous Power Denote and Their Relationship to the Gospel," in *The Kingdom and the Power: Are Healing and the Spiritual Gifts Used by Jesus and the Early Church Meant for the Church Today,* ed. Gary Greig and Kevin Springer, 133-174 (Ventura, CA: Regal Books, 1993). Wayne Grudem, "Should Christians Expect Miracles Today? Objections and Answers from the Bible," in *The Kindom and the Power; Are Healing and the Spiritual Gifts Used By Jesus and the Early Church Meant For the Church Today?,* ed. Gary Greig and Kevin Springer, 55-110 (Ventura, CA: Regal Books, 1993). Craig S. Keener, *Miracles: The Credibility of the New Testament Accounts* , 2 vols. (Grand Rapids, Michigan: Baker Academic, 2011). Especially Craig Keener, "Chapter 6 Developing Hume's Skepticism toward Miracles," in *Miracles: The Credibility of the New Testament Accounts,* 171-208 (Grand Rapids , MI: Baker Academic). George Eldon Ladd, *The Kingdom of God* (Carlisle: Paternoster Press, 1959). Vladimir Lossky, "The Mystical Theology of the Eastern Church" (St. Vladimir Seminary Press, 1997). Ramsay MacMullen, *Christianizing The Roman Empire A.D. 100-400* (New Haven, Connecticut: Yale University Press , 1984). Francis MacNutt, *Healing* (Notre Dame, IN: Ave Maria Press, 1974). Francis MacNutt, *The Healing Reawakening: Reclaiming Our Lost Inheritance*, Paper back edition printed 2006 Previously published under the title The Nearly Perfect Crime (Grand Rapids, MI: Chosen, 2005,2006). Also see *Biblical and Historical Answers to Cessationism* 6 part teaching DVD series available at www.globalawakeningstore.com

[6] River is a reference to the renewal movement that embraces healing, and is drawn from the river mentioned in Ezekiel 47:5-12 and Revelation 22:1 where in both passages it is a river of healing.

PART TWO

Streams that Feed the River
of Healing within Christianity

CHAPTER TWO

The Apostolic and Ante-Nicene Church

There is a great deal of prejudice within the Church regarding this "river of healing" that has been released on the earth by God, and much division has resulted. All too often we mistake the smaller stream we are in for the "River" itself, with a tendency to view the streams of others as foul or polluted, assuming that they don't flow into the River like our stream does. No valid stream is pure and without pollution from man, but it is important that we discern what is pollution from what is from God, and then work to clean up our individual stream so that all can receive the blessings intended by God.

As we learn to honor the streams flowing from our brothers and sisters in the Church that Jesus died to establish, and come into a place of greater unity as the body of Christ, I believe God will open the windows of heaven with His blessings.

Behold, how good and how pleasant it is for brothers to dwell together in unity! It is like the precious oil upon the head, coming down upon the beard, even Aaron's beard, coming down upon the edge of his robes. It is like the dew of Hermon coming down upon the mountains of Zion; for there the LORD commanded the blessing - life forever.

(Psalm 133 NASB)

Throughout the history of Christianity we have seen the development of these streams that feed the mighty river of healing within the Church. My knowledge of the streams within Orthodox and Coptic Christianity is insufficient to represent these two members of the family of Christianity; however, I do feel qualified to speak about six other streams, and so we shall examine those to see what positive contributions each brings to the river of healing within Christianity. As I mentioned earlier, I have personally experienced or been a part of almost all of these smaller streams.

The Apostolic Church and the Ante-Nicene Church Streams

During both the Apostolic period from 30 A.D. to mid 90 A.D., and the Ante-Nicene period from mid 90 A.D. to 325 A.D., which were about 300 years after the crucifixion and resurrection of Jesus, there were healings of all kinds of illnesses, deliverances, and the dead were raised. The models used by the early church were similar to the way Jesus ministered healing and raised the dead. From this time period we also see methods used that were based upon the actions of Elijah or Elisha in the Old Testament.

The miracles, signs and wonders, healings, and the raising of the dead were preceded by prayers of command rather than intercessory prayer. Those praying were not commanding God, but rather commanding the illness and the demonic sources behind the illness to leave. They understood the power and authority of His (Jesus') name and commanded healing in His name. We do not find on the lips of those early Christians the phrase used so often by many in the Church today, "If it be Your will."

During these first approximately three hundred years of the Church, an army of "nameless and faceless" Christians performed healings and deliverances. Though there were always those with greater gifts or anointing who were used more powerfully or more frequently, the ministry of healing was not limited to the Apostles or their immediate successors.

endnotes

[1] Ramsay MacMullen, *Christianizing The Roman Empire A.D. 100-400* (New Haven, Connecticut: Yale University Press , 1984). Michael Green, *Evangelism in the Early Church* (Grand Rapids, Michigan: William B. Eerdmans Publishing Company, 1970). Michael Green, *Evangelism in the Early Church* (Grand Rapids, Michigan: William B. Eerdmans Publishing Company, 1970, 2003), especially 263-272.

CHAPTER THREE

Roman Catholicism and Orthodox Healing Streams

As time progressed, especially after Emperor Constantine's Edict of Milan (313 A.D.) legalized the Christian faith, healings and other signs and wonders and miracles began to decrease. It is important to note that they decreased but they did not end, although they sometimes took on different formats within some of the different streams.

For example, in the Catholic Church it became very common for people to experience healing when praying at a reliquary, that place that houses the bones of those believed to be saints within the Catholic Church.

Another and more common means of healing that emerged was healing through the sacrament of the Eucharist. Some of the leading figures in the fight for orthodoxy took the "host" and rubbed it on their bodies to receive healing from life threatening conditions.[1] Father Michael Scanlan, a Catholic Priest and former President of a Catholic college says that when we receive the Eucharist we are given the gifts, in His body and blood, of both physical and spiritual healing, and empowered with the love of Christ and his wisdom and strength to face whatever may come our way.[2]

In addition to healing through the sacrament of the Eucharist, the Roman Catholic Church has a sacrament specifically for healing called "Unction" or "Anointing with Oil." This sacrament is based upon the scriptural admonition for the sick to call for the elders of the church to anoint them with oil (James 5:14). Father Scanlan and Sister Shields state,

> In the Anointing of the Sick, we can experience in our need the most loving thing God desires to do for us. We expect that to happen to us and to those for whom we gather to pray as they receive the sacrament. We expect to see the sick restored to health...we expect to see those [so] called [to] approach death with joy and total confidence. [3]

This sacrament is one of the seven sacraments in the Roman Catholic Church, and they believe, as do the Orthodox and Anglican traditions, that each one of these sacraments can be beneficial in bringing health to the body. The sacrament of "Unction" or "Anointing with Oil for Healing" was changed to "Last Rites" or "Extreme Unction" in the Middle Ages, but was changed back to "Anointing for Healing" by Vatican II (1962-1965).

Over time views developed within the Roman Catholic Church that brought about a paradigm shift that would have a negative impact on the ministry of healing. There was a transfer of power from the laity to clergy that emerged. Where once the laity could move in gifts of healing, now only very holy people could have the gift of healing. This understanding was not only unbiblical, but it became the basis for persecution within the Catholic Church. For example, if a "little ole me," a common person not known for their piety, began to move in the gift of healing or prophecy, they were often considered witches.

God's priesthood of believers, His army of believers who were commissioned to do His works and to do even greater works than Jesus (John 14:12), this army of disciples who were to be taught to do all the things that Jesus had commanded (Matthew 28:18-20), His army of "nameless and faceless," were replaced. They were replaced by those called to a religious vocation, namely the priests and the nuns and the brothers. It became dangerous for the laity, the non-religious and those without a religious vocation, to move in the gifts of the Spirit or in the power of the Holy Spirit.

In addition to this transfer of power from the laity to the clergy, two other lines of thinking developed within Roman Catholicism that would prove to be very detrimental to the ministry of healing. The first was that sickness was now somehow connected to the suffering verses in the Bible as a way of carrying the cross that Jesus told his disciples to carry. (Luke 9:23) Suffering from sickness was seen to be for God's redemptive purposes, and perhaps his most common one.

Additionally, a theological viewpoint emerged within Roman Catholicism that said being used of God to do something supra empirical or supernatural was a sign that authenticated the teaching or doctrine of the Church. Much division occurred in the Church as a result of the move from healing and miracles as part of the expression of the gospel to authentication of true doctrine as their primary purpose.[4] It is a division we can no longer afford in the twenty-first century as we face the last strongholds of the enemy in the 10-40 Window and its billions of Hindus, Buddhists, and Muslims. (The Hindus, Buddhists, and Muslims are not our enemy, but the Devil is our enemy.)

A Church unified in Spirit needs to arise. I am not speaking of a human attempt, of an ecumenism like the World Council of Churches and the National Council of Churches. What I am saying is that I believe Christian leaders and churches need to speak well of each other and work together to acknowledge the Holy Spirit in those outside their own denomination or branch of Christianity.

One last development within the Roman Catholic Church that proved detrimental to the expectation of healing was the paradigm shift that occurred when the Church moved from a warfare worldview to a blueprint worldview. This shift began with the teaching of Augustine who held a strong predestination view. Before Augustine, early Christians believed that the devil and his demons were at war against God and His angels and His Church. They understood that in war there are attacks and there are causalities. With the advent of the blueprint worldview, when something bad happened, instead of fighting against it, people become introspective, searching for a reason why God would allow something bad to happen and what redemptive purpose this event had in the life of the wounded one. People stopped praying against sickness because healing might be against the will of God for their lives, as if God had allowed the sickness to come upon them for their sanctification or some other disciplinary purpose.

This theological viewpoint has obvious implications. Those who believe in the blueprint worldview live in contradiction, seeking medical help for illness even though they believe God has brought their sickness about for His redemptive purposes.

The Effect on the Priests and the Worship Services

What impact would these Catholic theological views of healing have upon the liturgy of the church? Both the Roman Catholic and the Eastern Orthodox Churches had as one of their sacraments the "Anointing of the Sick," which could be given both in the church and outside the church building, however only a priest or a bishop could administer these sacraments. During the Middle Ages the Roman Catholic Church changed the meaning from "healing" to "preparing a person's soul for death." Though the Eastern Orthodox never discontinued their sacrament of healing, the Protestant movement would be much more influenced by the western Roman Catholic Church. As already mentioned, thanks to Vatican Council II (1962-1965) the Roman Catholic Church has a renewed emphasis upon healing in the sacrament of the "Anointing of the Sick."

When the Roman Catholic Church developed its view of miracles with the primary purpose being the evidence of true doctrine, the Protestant Movement followed suit. The New Testament perspective of miracles as a demonstration of the reality of the gospel of the Kingdom was replaced with "proof of doctrinal orthodoxy." This position would ultimately cause the Lutheran and Reformed denominations to become Cessationist. They actually went well beyond the positions of their founders Luther and Calvin. Calvin believed the gifts could occur in the Church when it was being planted in a region or country which was totally unevangelized. In this case gifts of healing and miracles, tongues, interpretation of tongues, and prophecy could reappear, however, once the Church was established these gifts would end. While Luther believed in healing and in some of the gifts, he over-reacted to the superstition that existed in the medieval Roman Catholic Church that had been mixed in with the miraculous. Luther wrote,

> I know of no worldly help to give. If the physicians are at a loss to find a remedy, you may be sure that it is not a case of ordinary melancholy. It must rather be an affliction that comes from the devil, and this must be counteracted by the power of Christ with the prayer of faith. This is what to do, and what we have been accustomed to do; for a cabinet-maker here was similarly afflicted with madness and we cured him by prayer in Christ's name. Accordingly you should proceed as follows: Go to him with a deacon and two or three good men. Confident that you as pastor of the place, are clothed with the authority of the ministerial office, lay your hands upon him and say, 'Peace be with you, dear brother, from God our Father and from our Lord Jesus Christ.' Thereupon repeat the Creed and the Lord's Prayer over him in a clear voice, and close with these words: 'O God, almighty Father, who has told us through thy Son, "Verily, verily I say unto you, Whatsoever ye ask the father in my name, he will give it you"…Then, when you depart, lay your hands upon the man again and say, 'These signs shall follow them that believe; they shall lay hands on the sick, and they shall recover." Do this three times once on each of three consecutive days." [5]

As demonstrated in Luther's writing, he was much more open to healing and the gifts than some Lutheran denominations are today. It is also true that the Reformed denominations are much more Cessationist than their founder John Calvin. The Baptist denominations, though not having their origins in the Reformed movement, but rather in the Anabaptist movement, still developed Reformed theology, excluding the Free-Will and the General Baptist who both have Armenian theologies rather than Reformed. Most Baptist denominations were and are Cessationist.

From his writings in the latter part of his life, Luther doesn't appear to be a Cessationist. He might be more appropriately considered a soft-cessationist, with scholars like Dr. Paul King and Dr. Eddie Hyatt seeing him as a "developing, yet equivocating supernaturalist."[6]

Hyatt challenges the Cessationist interpretation of Luther in his book 2,000 Years of Charismatic Christianity by pointing out that Luther's early negative remarks about the gifts are related to the abuses and misuses by the Zwickau prophets in the early part of the Reformation, and to the un-critical superstitiousness within Roman Catholicism.[7] Luther's theological viewpoint indicates he still believed in prophecy, healing, and deliverance. He saw people healed when he prayed for healing, and he even prophesied himself. He wrote, in his famous hymn, A Mighty Fortress Is Our God, "The Spirit and the gifts are ours."[8] He didn't think miracles were necessary today, but he did believe God still did miracles today. Initially Luther believed exorcism was no longer appropriate. He didn't believe we could cast out demons. This is indicated in his early catechism however, in later editions, he included exorcism as part of the baptismal rite.[9]

God loves His Church, including the Roman Catholic portion of His Church, and He is actively renewing it. I was surprised to learn how God was moving in the Roman Catholic Church prior to the birth of Pente-costalism, and how it [the Roman Catholic Church] was used of God in birthing the Pentecostal movement.

In 1967, shortly after Vatican II (1962-1965), when the Roman Catholic Church called for a new Pentecost, they experienced a powerful move of the Holy Spirit. One of the principle leaders during that time in the area of healing was Father Francis MacNutt. His book *Healing* is, I believe, one of the most influential books on the subject. He addresses the problematic issue of sickness as suffering, rather than understanding sickness as persecution for the faith as the meaning of suffering in the biblical texts. He also brings correction to the overemphasis on the redemptive value of suffering as a way of carrying the cross of Jesus. He was an important writer during the Roman Catholic Charismatic Renewal, and one of the major leaders in the ministry of healing.

The Roman Catholic Church doctrinally has a much more biblical view of healing than many Protestant denominations. It has never accepted the Cessationist view that the end of healing and miracles has occurred, yet there is a difference between the official teaching of the Church and the common experience for most priests, who never get to see the miraculous in the sense of healing and deliverance. They believe it happens but don't expect it in their life or their ministry or their local parish. I believe their heart longs to know the supernatural power of the Christ they so devotedly serve. What joy would fill their souls to see divine power heal their parishioners through their prayers. They secretly wish to hear testimonies today that bear witness to the testimonies of Jesus, Paul, and Peter, and the many other great saints in the history of their Church, but sadly, for most, their eyes never see the miraculous, their ears never hear these modern day testimonies.

Because of the absence of credible testimony, their hope has all but died to this heart-felt longing for the experience of the presence of the living Christ's power in their life and ministry and parish. So, the parish priest, served by the nuns and the brothers, continues on faithfully serving the people in his parish. But with no testimony to build hope and faith there is no sense of destiny to call them forward to proclaim an expectant message of healing power for physical and mental disease; no real confidence in Christ's power today to break the bonds of the addicted and demonized. Since there is no real expectation, the priests cannot bring a message to awaken their parishioners to the possibility of the supernatural power of God to work in the lives. They believe God can do these things and actually does do them, but as one Protestant radio host is quick to say, "These things are possible today, but they are not normative."

What affect has this lack of expectancy had upon the liturgy of the Catholic Church? It has produced, too often, a form of godliness without power. It has caused the Charisma to become routine, and created a tension between the hierarchy of the institution and the charismatically-endowed prophetic ministers who often become feared and forced out of the institution.

I believe a day is coming when the seminaries of the Roman Catholic Church and the Orthodox Church will have classes to train their clergy to heal, to deliver, to prophesy and interpret dreams; to hear the voice of God, and to equip the laity to do these things as well. I am afraid what I have written will be taken as too much of an absolutist position; that all Roman Catholic Churches and Roman Catholic priests are like those I have described here. I know this is not true. I have met priests who are on fire for God, who believe in healing and deliverance, and the gifts of the Spirit and the Baptism in the Spirit. It is just that these priests are more the exception than the norm within the Roman Catholic clergy, in my opinion.

endnotes

[5]   Theodore B. Tappert, ed. Luther: Letters of Spiritual Counsel, Vol. 18. Library of Christian Classics (Philadelphia: Westminster Press, n.d.), 52.

[6]   Taken from my email discussions with Dr. Paul King who is my Doctor of Ministry Mentor at United Theological Seminary and author of 10 books including *God's Healing Arsenal, Genuine Gold, Come Up Higher,* and *Only Believe.*

[7]   Eddie L. Hyatt, *2000 Years of Charismatic Christianity* (Charisma House, Lake May, FL, 2002).

[8]   Martin Luther, *A Mighty Fortress Is Our God,* 1529.

[9]   Taken from my email discussions with Dr. Paul King.

CHAPTER FOUR

The Historical Protestant Reformation Denominations and Their Healing Streams

Both John Calvin and Martin Luther, two of the major leaders of the Protestant Reformation faced challenges on two fronts. On one front, the Roman Catholic Church challenged the Protestant reformers with the argument that Roman Catholicism had miracles, and these miracles that continued throughout its history were evidence that authenticated the doctrine or teaching of the Roman Catholic Church. On another front was the left wing of the Reformation, the Anabaptists, who were basing authority upon subjective revelations or prophecies.

Then there was the Munster Rebellion, also called the Peasants Revolt, which caused great concern for the Lutherans. It was caused by prophetic revelations which said that God had a heart for the poor serfs and believed in the justice of throwing off the oppression of the Baron Lords. (This writer believes the revelation was accurate and consistent with the heart of God for the poor, as revealed in scripture, but the interpretation was incorrect, though Liberation theologians would agree with the interpretation, but not with the strategy of application. Liberation theologians would have wanted a viable military plan to be successful in the rebellion.) The Peasants Revolt resulted in the death of approximately 50,000 peasants.

As a result of this rebellion a derogatory term developed that is still used among Lutherans today, which is "Enthusiast" or "Enthusiasm," and gives a very negative opinion of interior or subjective experience. The Lutheran perspective is that experience is not to be trusted. They believe objective truth is the rock-solid basis upon which a relationship with God is to be established. The famous Lutheran position for authority, "Sola Scriptura – Sola Fide," which translates "only Scripture - only faith," must be understood for what it was – a wresting of authority from the "Tradition of the Church" and from personal subjective experiences (prophecies and other kinds of revelations) which were experiences of the enthusiasts.

The reaction of Calvin to these challenges to authority was to develop a Cessationist position which taught that true miracles were limited to the apostolic period within the Church. This theological position taught that the miracles that were reported as happening within Catholicism, and that had happened in the history of the Catholic Church after the deaths of the Apostles, were not true miracles. This Cessationist view believed that certain gifts of the Holy Spirit had ceased; tongues, interpretation of tongues, prophecy, healing, and the working of miracles. As indicated in chapter 3, Luther, was a soft-cessationist whose theology embraced prophecy, healing and deliverance as things that God still does but he didn't believe they were necessary for today. For many Protestants the belief that it is possible for the miraculous to occur today would be seen as adhering to the same gullible superstitions that pervade Catholicism. (The language of the last sentence reflects the mindset and language of a time of great animosity between Roman Catholics and Protestants, when the latter were being persecuted by the former, and some time later hundreds of thousands died in the religious wars between Roman Catholics and Protestants in Europe.)

Calvin did believe, however, that when the gospel was being preached to unreached groups of people, these gifts could be expected to occur to establish the Church among those unreached peoples. This is a belief of Calvin that many Calvinists are not aware of, causing them to be more Cessationist than Calvin himself. But Calvin's reasoning was consistent; since the purpose of miracles was to prove the truth of the message, when the message was being brought to an unreached people group, the miracles could appear again to verify the truth of the message to the non-Christian culture. Once the people heard the gospel and the Church was established, miracles would cease.

Though Calvin stated this concept, as time went on, the tradition that he began and the churches that sprang from it forgot about this possibility and Cessationist thinking prevailed. This does not mean that Lutherans or Calvinists no longer believe it is possible for God to sovereignly work a miracle or heal someone, or that the Holy Spirit died out, but that the aforementioned sign gifts of the Holy Spirit died out. God can still heal, but people no longer have the gift to heal.

A recent book titled *Who's Afraid of the Holy Spirit* by Daniel B. Wallace and M. James Sawyer,[1] two modified Cessationists from Dallas Theological Seminary, reflects this moderately Cessationist position. The problem with this position is that it works against strong faith or a real expectancy for God to answer our prayers. This position developed because biblical scholars began to realize the former hard-core Cessationist position was not grounded in the Bible but was a reaction to supposed abuses within Pentecostalism and the Charismatic Movement. They also realized there had been significant changes in science and philosophy and in biblical hermeneutics, and that there was too much evidence to the contrary, too much evidence that people were being healed and miracles were occurring.

Protestantism's Reformation denominations; Lutheranism, the Reformed, including Baptists, and the Anglicans, retained the Catholic view that sickness was the way to understand the passages of Scripture dealing with suffering. I have been shocked by some of the pastoral care books written for the Anglican Communion even as late as the 1700s and 1800s. In these passages there is a strong connection between sickness and sin, between God bringing the sickness upon the person in order to bring them into a greater holiness in their lives. Protestantism also carried into its doctrinal system from Catholicism the connection between miracles and correct doctrine, seeing the purpose of miracles as vindication of correct doctrine. This caused both the Roman Catholics and the Protestants to reject any miraculous accounts from those claiming to be Christians who were not part of their churches.

Like Roman Catholicism that had adopted the blueprint worldview, after 430 A.D., the Protestant movement, primarily due to St. Augustine's influence, did not see this as something that needed to be reformed, especially since Luther was an Augustinian monk and was heavily influence by Augustine's writings. It is sad that Luther did not reject the blueprint worldview in his 95 Thesis. In the last fifty years this viewpoint has been challenged, especially within the past ten years.

When it came to healing, the Lutherans and Calvinists (Reformed, Presbyterians, and Baptists) adopted most of the theological views that had developed within Catholicism about suffering and sickness and gifts lost to the laity (and the clergy for protestants). They viewed sickness as a means of entering into the sufferings of Jesus, or carrying our cross, and the blueprint worldview that everything that happens is the will of God or at least His permissive will. But they went even further, stating that the "sign gifts" had ended, meaning that the gifts of miracles, healings, tongues, interpretation of tongues, and prophecy do not happen today.

The Impact Upon the Pastors and the Worship Service

What impact did these theological viewpoints have upon the liturgy or order of service in these denominations, and what impact did this have upon the average person in the pew? First, strong prayers of faith became intercessory prayers. Where there had once been prayers of command or declarations of commands, there were now intercessory prayers on behalf of another, asking God to have mercy and heal, *if* it was His will.

Now, instead of being with the sick person, laying hands on them and anointing him or her with oil, the person praying usually prayed from a distance, often at the church. Pastoral prayers for the sick from the safety of the pulpit replaced the elders going to the sick person, anointing them with oil and praying the prayer of faith. More frequently, the prayers for the sick went something like this: "God, please guide the surgeon's hand," or "God please comfort the sick in their sickness," or "God be with the family during this time of sickness," and "Lord strengthen them and speed up their recovery."

These kinds of pastoral prayers and congregational prayers or prayers for those on the "prayer list" replaced prayers of faith that addressed the illness or condition itself and commanded it to be healed in Jesus' name. Even when on occasion the Elders did go to pray, it was usually not with an expectation that the person would recover in response to their prayers as much as it was to comfort the person through their visit. The clergy sometimes unintentionally began to pray for the ears of the sick to hear and be comforted, more than for the ears of God to hear and act, to intervene and to respond not only with persevering strength but also preferably with power to heal.

Having considered the implications of the Cessationist view from a liturgical viewpoint, let us now turn for a moment and consider some of the implications from a pastoral viewpoint.

First, the Cessationist position regarding healing does not require the pastor to take risks to try and discern whether or not what he believes he is sensing is truly illumination from the inspiration of the Spirit to pray for a certain condition or for the sick at a particular time in the service. It eliminates the need to step out in faith and risk being wrong or looking foolish to others. It is a safe position but allows no room for pastors to grow. The prophet said it this way, *"Where no oxen are, the crib is clean; but much increase is by the strength of the ox"* (Proverbs 14:4).

The second implication or ramification of the Cessationist position for pastors is that when they don't take risks with the Holy Spirit, they don't learn how to develop their spiritual gifts. They don't have to learn how to recognize the different ways the Triune God communicates with them. They can rely upon their own abilities and the training they received in Bible college or seminary, or from a human mentor, but in so doing they miss the excitement of being mentored by the Holy Spirit in regard to "hearing and healing." Paul wrote in 2 Corinthians 4:13,

It is written: "I believed; therefore I have spoken." With that same spirit of faith we also believe and therefore speak. (NIV)

This hearing and doing is a major theme in the Upper Room discourse of Jesus in John 14-16. This type of speaking that is based upon believing, which comes from revelation from the Holy Spirit, does not occur according to the Cessationist, especially in regard to operating in gifts of healings, and so it follows that there is little effort to see a breakthrough or to grow in the area of healing, either individually as a pastor, or to help the laity grow in the operation of these gifts. Yet, like the Roman Catholic priests, I believe these wonderful servants of God would love to experience the power to heal, would love for their eyes to see the manifest power of God heal someone or deliver someone, and would love to hear the testimony of the deeds of God done in our time, but the Cessationist belief system works against them.

endnotes

[1] Daniel B. Wallace, and M. James Sawyer, ed., *Who's Afraid of the Holy Spirit?*, ed. Daniel B. Wallace and M. James Sawyer (Dallas, Texas: Biblical Studies Press, 2005).

the healing river

CHAPTER FIVE

The Anglican and Episcopal Church Streams

Anglicanism has often been referred to as the middle way between Catholicism and Protestantism. Sometimes called "Anglo-Catholic," it is not in fact part of the Roman Catholic Church.

As I mentioned earlier, I have read some disheartening statements from the *Book of Common Prayer* of the Church of England in regards to healing. We will examine some lengthy quotes from *The Book of Common Prayer* that was written in the 1500's and is still used today by some churches, although the 1979 revised version is seen as the more preferable version for the majority of churches within the Episcopal and Anglican communes in the twenty-first century. The quote below is from the English Office of the Visitation of the Sick:

When any person is sick, notice shall be given thereof to the Minister of the Parish; who coming into the sick person's house, shall say ..." The minister – when ministers used the Office – then began by invoking God's mercy upon the miserable sufferer, and after invoking the Lord's Prayer and a few versicles and response, he went on:[1]

Hear us, Almighty and most merciful God and Savior; extend thy accustomed goodness to this thy servant who is grieved with sickness. . . . Sanctify, we beseech thee, this thy fatherly correction to him; that the sense of his weakness may add strength to his faith, and seriousness to his repentance: That, if it shall by thy good pleasure to restore him to his former health, he may lead the residue of his life in thy fear, and to thy glory: or else, give him grace so to take thy visitation, that, after this painful life is ended, he may dwell with thee in life everlasting; through Jesus Christ our Lord.[2]

If the person was considered to be so sick that they couldn't listen to more the Minister would stop, but if the person was of good enough health to pay attention to more the Minister continued.

Dearly beloved, know this, that Almighty God is the Lord of life and death, and of all things to them pertaining, as youth, strength, health, age, weakness, and sickness. Wherefore, whatsoever your sickness is, know you certainly that it is god's visitation. And for what cause soever this sickness is sent unto you; whether it be to try your patience for the example of others, and that your faith may be found in the day of the Lord laudable, glorious, and honourable, to the increase of glory and endless felicity; or else it be sent unto you to correct and amend in you whatsoever doth offend the eyes of your heavenly Father; know you certainly, that if you truly repent you of your sins, and bear your sickness patiently, trusting in God's mercy, for his dear Son Jesus Christ's sake, and submitting yourself wholly unto his will, it shall turn to your profit, and help you forward in the right way that leadeth unto everlasting life.

The above passage was read to those who were very ill, possibly with terminal illness, but, if the person had a probable hope of living the Minister would continue by reading the following advice to him or her:

Take therefore in good part the chastisement of the Lord: For (as

Saint Paul saith in the twelfth Chapter to the Hebrews) whom
the Lord loveth he chasteneth, and scourgeth every son whom he
receiveth. If ye endure chastening, God dealeth with you as with
sons; for what son is he whom the father chasteneth not? But if ye
be without chastisement, whereof all are partakers, then are ye
bastards, and not sons. Furthermore, we have had fathers of our
flesh, which corrected us, and we gave them reverence; shall we not
much rather be in subjection unto the Father of spirits, and live? For
they verily for a few days chastened us after their own pleasure; but
be for our profit, that we might be partakers of his holiness. These
words, good brother, are written in holy Scripture for our comfort and
instruction; that we should patiently, and with thanksgiving, bear our
heavenly Father's correction, whensoever by any manner of adversi-
ty it shall please his gracious goodness to visit us. And there should
be no greater comfort to Christian persons, than to be made like unto
Christ, by suffering patiently adversities, troubles, and sicknesses. For he himself went not up to joy, but first he suffered pain; he
entered not into his glory before he was crucified. So truly our way
to eternal joy is to suffer here with Christ; and our door to enter into
eternal life is gladly to die with Christ; that we may rise again from
death, and dwell with Him in everlasting life. Now therefore, taking
your sickness, which is thus profitable for you patiently, I exhort
you, in the name of God, to remember the profession which you
made unto God in your Baptism. And forasmuch as after this life
there is an account to be given unto the righteous Judge, by whom
all must be judged, without respect of persons, I require you to examine yourself and your estate, both towards God and man; so that,
accusing and condemning yourself for your own faults, you may find
mercy at our heavenly Father's hand for Christ's sake, and not be
accused and condemned in that fearful judgment. Therefore I shall
rehearse to you the Articles of our Faith, that you may know whether
you do believe as a Christian man should, or no.[3]

In 1854 a book was prepared to help the clergy with their pastoral ministry to the sick titled *Visitatio Infirmorum*. It has over 800 pages and contains penitential Psalms and suggestions for almost every kind of affliction or problem; however it still had the flavor of the earlier Book of Common Prayer. One of the longer forms of examination called the Trail and Judgment of the Soul, begins,

> Are you persuaded that your present sickness is sent unto you by Almighty GOD? ... And that all which you now suffer is far less than you have deserved to suffer? . . . Are you fully sensible and convinced now, how little there is in (all your possessions), and how soon you may be, or are like to be taken to them?

This type of questioning was but one of many such questions, and was used for the actual examination of sick people in any condition short of dying. In 1928 the American Episcopal Church removed the two passages, but the passages of Scripture used for the newer service indicate that there is still a strong influence of this kind of theological viewpoint. For instance, there is this quote from Episcopal scholar Kelsey:

> The idea of sickness as a time to catch a person and get his conscience and his ideas of faith straightened out intellectually is still to be found.[4]

This quote reveals the reasoning of the blueprint worldview that St. Augustine introduced into the theology of the Church, leading the people of the Church away from the warfare worldview. Now it is seen to be a holy thing to accept sickness as from God rather than fight against sickness as an attack from the powers of darkness.

I believe it would be easy to find in the United States many Episcopalians and Anglicans who do not believe in healing and do not practice healing, while in much of the third world the Anglican clergy understand and believe in the warfare worldview and see sickness as coming from the devil, ultimately caused by individual sins, sins against the sick person, or the original sin of the Fall, and as such to be fought against. We must remember what Peter said about the ministry of Jesus in Acts 10:37-38:

You know what has happened throughout Judea, beginning in Galilee after the baptism that John preached— how God anointed Jesus of Nazareth with the Holy Spirit and power, and how he went around doing good and healing all who were under the power of the devil, because God was with him.

It was clear to the Apostles that Jesus, the incarnation of God, came to destroy sickness through healing, and that disease was somehow connected to the power of the devil and not caused by God.

In the United States the work of an Episcopal priest, Dr. Morton Kelsey, has been instrumental in understanding the relationship between Christian history and the role of healing in that history. John Wimber and I were both impacted by the writings of Dr. Kelsey and Dr. Francis MacNutt on healing. Dr. MacNutt left the Roman Catholic Church and became an Episcopalian priest when he married. (MacNutt has since been received back into the Roman Catholic Church and teaches on healing within it with Vatican approval.) I had read their works prior to meeting John Wimber and when I read John's acknowledgment in the front of one of the booklets that accompanied his audio teaching series on healing, I knew I had found a kindred spirit. The Anglican cleric, Nikki Gumble's Alpha Course, which has recognizable influences from Wimber, has had tremendous impact upon the larger Anglican Church, especially in relation to the Holy Spirit and His gifts.

Then there is The International Order of St. Luke the Physician in the United States, which is committed to furthering a healthy model for healing within the Episcopal and Anglican Church. This organization represents a very healthy expression of healing. Its reading list is quite well balanced.[5] One of the best books I have read that brings balance to the issue of healing, especially for the more liturgical church, was written by Episcopal priest Mark Pearson and titled *Christian Healing*.[6]

Another person of note from the Episcopal/Anglican stream that bears mention is the Reverend Terry Fullam who was an Episcopal Charismatic leader of the mid-twentieth century in America and a disciple of Dennis Bennett. His church in Connecticut came alive in the power of the Holy Spirit and experienced a renewal that moved beyond its walls to impact others who were being touched by God with renewal fire. Although healing was not the focus of Fullam's ministry, what God did through him in Darien and beyond gave encouragement to those in Episcopal Church in the 1970s who were being led into the ministry of healing, such as Kelsey, Francis and Judith MacNutt, Mike Evans, and Mark Pearson.

I have friends whose experiences also highlight what has been happening in the last few decades in regards to healing in some churches within the Episcopal/Anglican stream. Baptized in the spirit at an Episcopal retreat by Mike Evans, they spent the next ten years in an Episcopal congregation in which the gifts were allowed to flow freely and healing was a normal part of the Sunday service. That particular congregation had a strong connection to the Episcopal Church in Uganda.

These friends have watched healing ministries rise up within several local Anglican churches in the Washington, D.C. area, and through this network of churches they have trained under Judith and Francis MacNutt, David and Mary Pytches, Mike Evans, and LeAnne Payne. David and Mary Pitches' church, St. Andrew's in Chorleywood, England experienced revival when the spirit of God fell on them during a visit from John Wimber and his team. Out of this experience came David's first book, *Come Holy Spirit*, which is "based on the teaching and practical outworking of the ministry in the power of the Holy Spirit." David and Mary served for seventeen years as missionaries in Chile, and in South America, and in 1970 he became bishop there.[7] The Pitches continue to minister in the power of the Holy Spirit around the globe.

The Impact Upon the Pastors and the Liturgy

The liturgical implications for healing are different within different Anglican and Episcopal churches depending on whether they are high-church or low-church and what continent they are on. It would be unusual for many Episcopal or Anglican churches to have services for healing or to dedicate a portion of their regular Sunday service for healing prayer.

Pastoral implications for the Anglican denominations vary. Overall, the Anglican approach is more of a reserved approach in contrast to the emotionalism of the Pentecostal or Charismatic denominations, and more open to the insights of psychology and psychotherapy than other Pentecostal and Charismatic models. There is also a greater emphasis upon the sacrament of healing and the Eucharist or Lord's Supper than found in most Pentecostal or Charismatic churches, which doesn't necessarily look too different from the integrated model that was developed by John Wimber and which I now teach all over the world.

Again, the average pastor in the Episcopal/Anglican stream most likely did not receive any training in seminary regarding healing, hearing from the Lord, prophecy, words of knowledge and the operation of faith for healing, or the gift of faith for the working of miracles. Because these pastors have little experience or knowledge of these things they often feel uncomfortable facilitating any opportunities for healing in their services. The denominational position that has been Cessationist for so long can take years to overcome, and it could be years before congregations develop a comfort level and openness to a liturgy that has a place in it for healing.

I pray for the in-breaking of the Holy Spirit to continue in the Episcopal and Anglican streams in regards to healing, and for their clergy to be trained and raised up to move in the gifts of healing and to equip their laity. I am certain that, like their Roman Catholic counterparts, many of these Anglican and Episcopal bishops and pastors long to experience the power to heal and to see that power manifest in the lives of those they lovingly shepherd.

Let us now turn our attention from these liturgical denominations to the Faith Cure and Word of Faith streams that grew out of the holiness movement, which has its roots in the teachings of John Wesley and his followers.

endnotes

[1]   Morton Kelsey, *Healing and Christianity* (San Francisco, CA: Harper and Row Publishers reprinted Augsburg Fortress, 1973, 1995 Augsburg Fortress Edition, 15-17.

[2]   (Italics are Kelsey's, bold the author's.)

[3]   Ibid., 15-18.

[4]   Ibid., 19.

[5]   www.orderofstluke.org

[6]   Mark Pearson, *Christian Healing: A Comprehensive and Practical Guide* (Lake Mary, FL: Charisma House, 2004).

[7]   http://anglicanroots.org/Pytches.htm

the healing river

CHAPTER SIX

The Faith Cure and Word of Faith Streams

Both the Faith Cure movement and the Word of Faith movement are related in their teachings. The earlier Faith Cure movement has definitely affected the latter Word of Faith movement through the writings and personal connections between the two. I believe these movements have been the most maligned and misunderstood of any Christian expression of healing. I believe there are two reasons for the misunderstandings and negative images that exist of this stream.

The first reason is two-fold. There are extreme forms taken by some of the preachers and teachers from within the movements that have placed too great an emphasis upon prosperity. Add to that a harshness that exists, making people feel condemned if they honestly admit they would like someone to pray for them because their healing hasn't "manifested yet."

The second reason for so much misunderstanding and so many inaccurate statements about these movements is the poor historical research by D. R. McConnell in his book *A Different Gospel*,[1] which has been quoted by many, even the scholarly *Dictionary of Pentecostal and Charismatic Movements*.[2]

As stated earlier, I want to build bridges not walls between the various healing streams that make up the healing river of God. Before I try to bring forth the positive aspects from the Faith Cure and Word of Faith streams I want to state where I am coming from. When I first became acquainted with the Charismatic Movement I lived near Louisville, Kentucky. From time to time I would visit a strong charismatic Southern Baptist Church, and a very healthy Roman Catholic prayer group. I had read Francis MacNutt's *Healing*,[3] Morton Kelsey's *Healing and Christianity*,[4] and Robert Culpepper's book, *Evaluating the Charismatic Movement*.[5] Culpepper was a Southern Baptist professor of theology in Japan for the Foreign Mission Board of the Southern Baptist Convention when he wrote the book. I was very open and impressed by these writings. Furthermore, while in college and seminary, the Holy Spirit strongly impressed upon me that "the issue of my lifetime would be the Holy Spirit." I studied, as much as possible, issues related to the Holy Spirit and to the Charismatic Movement and healing while in school and I felt very positive about the Charismatic Movement I experienced during my seminary years.

When I graduated from seminary and began pastoring full time in Illinois I experienced a side of the Charismatic Movement I had not seen before, namely the Word of Faith movement. What I saw was not the best expression of that movement, but a rather poor expression of it. Negative statements brought condemnation, and an emphasis upon being a person of faith was demonstrated by having such things as a Rolex watch, or an expensive car or home, and wearing expensive clothes. I saw more condemnation than love, which caused me to back away from this expression of the Charismatic Movement for a season.

In October 1994, in Ontario, Canada, my wife DeAnne and I were at a meeting with John and Carol Arnott, Wes and Stacey Campbell, and Mark DuPont. We had come together to pray and fellowship. During this time Mark DuPont gave me a prophetic word which soon came to pass. It had come to him in a vision. The word was encouraging and part of it was,

> Your ministry is about to change. You are about to begin ministering with the Pentecostals, Assemblies of God, and Word of Faith. And, I

know your testimony; I know that the last one will be hard for you to accept, but in the near future God is going to open to you a door to the Pentecostals, Assemblies, and the Word of Faith.

My response was, "If that happens it will have to be God. I don't know any Pentecostals, my theology isn't classical Pentecostal, and I don't even like the Word of Faith Movement. It would be a miracle if that happened!"

Up until that time all my invitations were coming from the Vineyard. After this prophecy the invitations immediately went from 100% Vineyard to 10% Vineyard. They were now also coming from Pentecostals, Charismatics, Word of Faith, and some large Baptist, Lutheran, Roman Catholic, and Independent Churches, but the majority of invitations were from the Pentecostals, Charismatics and Assemblies of God.

During this time God was teaching me things. He showed me that I needed to repent for all the mean-spirited things I had said about the Word of Faith Movement, and that I was to go to the leaders of the Rhema Church in Tulsa where I had encountered Rodney Howard-Browne and ask for forgiveness. I did just that, and I told them I wouldn't speak badly about them anymore.

Even though God had dealt with my spirit on this I still thought my theology was right and Word of Faith's was wrong, or at the very least unhealthy. My thinking came out of my experiences with the Word of Faith message. I had seen the negative but now God was going to let me see the positive. He arranged it so that I kept hearing testimonies from people who had received a significant healing after confessing the promises of God. For a while it seemed like everywhere I went I kept meeting Word of Faith people who had been healed of terminal illness by standing in faith.

Somewhere around 1999 I began to question the position on healing that I had been so comfortable with in the Vineyard. I began to see that the "kingdom now-not yet" teaching was actually lowering people's expectation for healing. I also began to realize that there had been other more powerful movements and personalities that had seen more healings than John Wimber, and almost all of them believed healing was both in the cross of Jesus as well as His Kingdom. "Kingdom now-not yet" theology was actually only a step away from saying that healing is determined by the sovereignty of God.

I became convinced that God was much more willing to heal than our experiences demonstrated. I also thought that the Vineyard and Third Wave Evangelicals were too easily convinced God was not doing anything if they did not see some type of manifestation, or if the person did not feel anything when they prayed for someone. We had learned how to recognize the effects of the Holy Spirit upon the body, and if we did not see those phenomena we often assumed God was not doing anything in the person.

Then in 2003, I met Joe McIntyre. Joe was an apostolic leader in the Word of Faith Movement. Bill Johnson gave me Joe's book to read, *E.W. Kenyon and His Message of Faith: The True Story.* I read it twice including every footnote. Many false understandings I had about Word of Faith teaching were corrected as a result of reading this book. I gained a true historical understanding of the origins of the confession-possession teaching. I discovered it was not rooted in New Thought, Unity, or Christian Science, but rather was rooted in the best teaching among evangelicals in the latter half of the 19th century; men like D.L. Moody, R.A. Torrey, A. J. Gordon, A.B. Simpson, George Mueller, and others.

I learned Word of Faith was actually rooted in the 19th century holiness movement and the shorter way to sanctification as taught by Mrs. Palmer. She taught that the way to enter into sanctification was to receive it by faith and confess it as true until it manifested in your life. She understood that the way we receive justification is the same way we receive sanctification; by faith apart from feelings, and with the confession of our lips to the reality. Both are benefits to us through the cross of Jesus. We only need take one more step to move from justification and sanctification to the belief that we receive healing by trusting, believing in the covenant promises of God provided in the cross of Jesus, and confessing those promises as already received, while waiting patiently for the manifestation of faith's confession. This isn't sensory denial, but the confession of a greater truth than what is being physically experienced at the moment of prayer. It isn't denying truth but merely believing in a greater truth.

In long phone discussions and later in personal discussions with Joe, I was able to see that my real issue was not with the Word of Faith message, but with the poor pastoral applications of this message which caused people to feel badly about their faith and themselves if they were not healed. It was that and the overemphasis upon prosperity that was becoming all too common in the movement that had been stumbling blocks for me.

I soon discovered that I had spoken the wrong words from my pulpit about the Word of Faith movement. I had the wrong impressions about the movement from my limited experience, and I had received incorrect information from faulty sources that purported to be scholarly. These faulty sources based their historical research upon positions that were incorrectly formed. Joe's book proved beyond doubt that McConnell's book, *Another Gospel*, was historically inaccurate, and his conclusions about Kenyon being influenced by the metaphysical movement of the 19th century was also inaccurate. His conclusions were based upon an assumption that Kenyon was influenced by New Thought which is not true. McConnell's research was poor regarding the historical timeline in Kenyon's life. This timeline was critical for his thesis of New Thought influence.

I believe that there is truth in the Word of Faith message. To use one of John Wimber's favorite metaphors, I would say that it [the Word of Faith message] is one of the golf clubs we need in our bag to be more successful in our game. There will be times when we need to pull this club out and use it. For this reason I now often have Pastor Joe McIntyre teach a more balanced presentation on healing from the Faith Camp perspective in my Schools of Healing and Impartation. I want to bring balance to the "now-not yet" theology of healing that is rooted in the position that healing is in the Kingdom of God, which is both now and not yet.

In addition I have had Dr. Paul King teach a School of Healing and Impartation for me called *Foundations of Faith*. Dr. King, Joe McIntyre and I taught this school for the first time in 2012. Dr. King helped us see the better version of this message of faith, comparing the critics' accusations to the actual teachings of both the Faith Cure movement and the Word of Faith movement. Dr. King's book, *Only Believe: Examining the Origin and Development of Classic and Contemporary "Word of Faith" Theologies*, brings balance to McConnell and Word of Faith critics.[6] He pointed out positive insights gained through both movements. Joe McIntyre brought insight and a depth of understanding to this topic as well as clearing up the misunderstanding of the timeline of Kenyon's life as portrayed by McConnell.

We can choose to judge any of these streams by their worst representatives or their best representatives. We can decide to illustrate the lack of balance by stories that are nightmarish, boarding on the ludicrous, and even embarrassing to other leaders in the Word of Faith Movement, or we can illustrate the balance within the movement with wonderful stories of the dead being raised, the terminally ill healed, and confidence restored in those who have been torn down emotionally and spiritually.

While others have attempted to judge a movement by its roots rather than its fruits, choosing not to follow Jesus' advice for discernment, we should be careful not to make the same mistake. This mistaken judgment has done damage to the Word of Faith Movement by incorrectly connecting it to New Thought, Theosophy, and Christian Science, through E.W. Kenyon's supposed connection with these groups. But, as we already have shown, the roots of Kenyon are in the teachings of some of the greatest Evangelical teachers of the last half of the 19th century rather than the New Thought cults.[7]

The Faith Cure movement predated both the metaphysical movement and Christian Science. The leaders of Faith Cure were adamantly against the philosophical understanding of both, seeing both as heretical and speaking against them. I discovered that Kenyon was influenced the most by the Baptist A. J. Gordon, and indirectly by George Peck, the author of *Throne Life*. This book powerfully influenced A. J. Gordon, with an emphasis upon the "finished work" of Christ for sanctification, and the basis for our authority to be seated with Christ in heavenly places with all things put under his feet.

Gordon's teaching would influence Kenyon regarding the "finished work" with an understanding that is the Pauline understanding of the gospel. Kenyon would then influence William Durham with the "finished work" message that would then influence the Pentecostal movements, including the Assemblies of God. This would cause the Assemblies of God, a Pentecostal denomination, at one of their formative meetings, to reject the more Wesleyan concept of sanctification and holiness for the Keswickian understanding of appropriation by faith, apart from feeling, based upon the positive confession of the promises of God in the finished work of Christ.

Once this logical step of appropriating the work of Christ for forgiveness and justification was seen to be the way to appropriate sanctification, it was not long before it was seen to be the way to appropriate healing. How; by a positive confession by faith of what the promises of Scripture offer in the finished work of Christ's crucifixion, resurrection, and ascension, and believing that we have received these promises until the healing that happened on the cross of Christ manifests physically in our body. The way to enter into salvation is the way to receive sanctification, and the way to receive healing.

The Faith Cure Movement did not have an emphasis upon the gifts of healing, the anointing for healing, or healing evangelists. Those would enter the Church later. Its emphasis was upon understanding the promises of Scripture regarding healing, believing in those promises, understanding our right to come and receive because of our covenant with God, and appropriating by confession the healing before it manifests, as having been already accomplished in Christ at the Cross, until it manifests in our physical bodies through the life of Christ that is in us.

The Faith Cure movement had strong leaders, scholarly men of the word of God. A. J. Gordon, for example, read the Bible every morning in Greek for his devotionals. B. B. Warfield would devote a whole chapter of his book, *Counterfeit Miracles*, in an attempt to refute Gordon's book on healing and miracles.[8] Warfield did not even address the Pentecostal movement in his book.

Sadly, the negative view of medicine held by most of the people in the Faith Cure movement would cause it to lose its popularity and favor among the American Christian community. This negative view of medicine and the birth of Pentecostalism that immediately accepted the teaching about healing held by the Faith Cure Movement would cause most Evangelicals to reject the message of healing because of its opposition to the Pentecostal Movement. With the vehement rejection of Pentecostalism by Evangelicalism, healing came to be seen as a Pentecostal teaching rather than an Evangelical rediscovery, which it truly was.

E. W. Kenyon became a major connection between the Faith Cure movement and the Word of Faith Movement, as well as some of the early Pentecostal Healing Evangelists. For example, T. L. Osborne dedicates his classic book on healing to Kenyon.[9] Kenyon's writings were very influential upon later Word of Faith teachers. It is interesting that Kenyon did not join the Pentecostal Movement; he remained a Free Will Baptist.

The classic book written by F.F. Bosworth, *Christ the Healer*, was the summation of the doctrinal teaching of the Faith Cure movement regarding healing. It too became a most important book for the new Pentecostal movement. As demonstrated later, the Pentecostal movement emphasized the restoration of the gifts of the Spirit, something the Faith Cure movement did not do. Unlike the Pentecostals, those in the Faith Cure movement did not see that movement as God restoring the charismatic gifts of the Spirit to the church, nor the restoration of the offices of Ephesians 4. I realize that many Pentecostals, in their reaction to the Latter Rain, movement would chaff at my last sentence, but I cannot read the early writings of Pentecostalism without seeing an embrace of apostolic and prophetic ministry within early Pentecostalism.

The Effect on the Pastors and Worship Services

What impact would Word of Faith have upon the actual church

service, the worship liturgy? Very little; there would not be an emphasis upon coming forward for prayer from someone else because the emphasis was not upon the gift of healing or upon an anointed healer, but rather the emphasis was upon appropriating healing through faith in God's biblical promises regarding healing.

How would Faith Cure affect the ministry of the pastor? For one thing, pastors wouldn't have a completely Cessationist viewpoint anymore. Instead, they found it important to teach Biblical promises regarding healing; Biblical promises that encompassed how to appropriate healing, faith, covenant, the relationship of God's sovereignty, and the revelation of His will through His covenantal promises. And more importantly, they would teach about who we are in Christ - the effects of Christ in us and the delegated authority we now have. They would discover the importance of teaching in order to establish faith in God's faithfulness, and in His promises, and in all that belongs to the believer through the finished work of Christ.

In some ways there would be parallels between Luther's rediscovery of justification by faith for salvation and Word of Faith's teaching on healing by faith. Both are received by faith, and faith is strengthened by a strong understanding that we are established in grace, not works, and not scripture memorization, but in relational trust in the goodness of God and the work of Jesus.

I believe most Word of Faith pastors and teachers today would identify with the Pentecostal and Charismatic movements, and would also be open to the truths about the gifts of healing and the anointing to heal, but with more emphasis upon the sick taking responsibility to receive their healing. It is interesting that some of the books written by professors of medicine today use more sophisticated language than "confess it, possess it," as they give credence to the power in faith.

Dr. Herbert Benson, in his book, *Timeless Healing*, uses the term "cognitive restructuring," and gives it a meaning which is very similar to what Word of Faith and Faith Cure give to their understanding of "confession and possession." Cognitive restructuring does not deny the reality of the condition of the body, but envisions a better option, a greater reality that can overcome the diseased reality. Dr. Benson who is a Professor of Medicine at Harvard Medical School writes,

> . . . Our minds are conditioned to react in certain ways, the wiring of our brains formed when we repeatedly call upon particular memories or thoughts and their signature neurons and neuron combinations.
>
> Because the brain is ever changing, we have the ability to rewire and modify those automatic reactions in a process sometimes called "cognitive restructuring." In fact, *the very act of reading these words* – the brain processing, incorporating, and integrating their meaning – is forever changing your brain's wiring. Every new experience, every new fact entered into your brain changes its configuration and you're awareness and understanding of who you were, who you are, and who you will be. Because of the brain's intrinsic malleability, you have the opportunity to literally "change your mind."
>
> In all the activities I am about to recommend, the goal is not to deny reality, only to project images and ideas of something better for you. You act "as if" the preferred reality was true and the body responds.[10]

There are many positive contributions from this stream to the healing river of God. There is the strong biblical stance of the movement to build its beliefs upon the Bible. There is the emphasis upon the believer believing or taking some responsibility to receive their healing. There is faith in the promises of God; grounding our faith in the will of God for healing; placing healing in the covenant of grace – making it available through grace and not a mechanical manipulation of God, but a trusting in the goodness and grace in the Fatherhood of God. And there is the aspect of understanding our authority to fight against sickness and disease as well as demonic based afflictions.

In my experience as a pastor I have found that the Faith Cure and Word of Faith stream brings great comfort to those people who have been to healing meetings where no word of knowledge ever came to them regarding their sickness, or even if it did, if they were not healed. In this stream they still find reason to hope. Or those who have gone to a classic

Pentecostal service where the emphasis was upon the anointed man or woman of God, and where someone might have laid hands upon them and prayed the prayer of faith and yet they were not healed. This stream gives them faith. Or those dear ones who were put on the prayer list at their local church which prays for sovereign healings, but they have not been healed.

I believe that the Word of Faith and Faith Cure streams give hope; hope not in a word of knowledge, or in an anointed evangelist, or the prayers of others, but in the promises of God, and His covenant; and though the answer seems to be delayed, it is still possible.

A few years ago I had a conversation with Helen, one of the members of my former church, the Vineyard church that my wife DeAnne and I started. Helen and her husband Bill were the first two people to join us in starting the church. She and Bill still attend this church. Helen is a precious saint. For the sixteen years that I was their pastor this dear couple were like parents to me in many ways. Age was beginning to take its toll on Helen's body, and she was battling illness on many fronts. She battled the physical and the emotional. Bouts of depression caused by long battles with the pain of fibromyalgia were weighing heavily on her soul.

One day, years after I resigned the church, Helen and I were talking on the phone. She told me she had never been healed by a word of knowledge, nor by the prayers of some "super anointed person." (We had many famous people visit our church to minister during the last eight years of my pastorate.) There had been no gift of healing to relieve her of her suffering. Helen's basis of hope was the promises of the Bible in regard to healing. Without this hope life would have been even darker during these bouts of fighting the good fight of faith on two fronts. For her the Word of Faith message was a rock to hold onto, to keep from drowning in despair, yet she would not consider herself a person who identifies with the Word of Faith movement. But, for this season of her life it is the "golf club" most beneficial to Helen in her situation. We need all the insights from the various streams that make up the Healing River, or to switch metaphors, we need all the golf clubs in our bag for the ministry of healing.

endnotes

[1] D. R. A McConnell, *Different Gospel: Biblical and Historical Insights into the Word of Faith Movement* (Peabody, MA: Hendrickson Publishers, 1995).

[2] Gary B. McGee, Patrick H. Alexander, and Stanley M. Burgess, ed., *Dictionary of Pentecostal and Charismatic Movements*, ed. (Grand Rapids, MI: Zondervan, 1988).

[3] Francis MacNutt, *Healing* (Notre Dame, IN: Ave Maria Press, 1974).

[4] Kelsey, *Healing and Christianity*.

[5] Robert Culpepper, *An Evaluation of the Charismatic Movement: A Theological and Biblical Appraisal* (Valley Forge, PA: Judson Press, 1977).

[6] Paul L. King, *Only Believe: Examining the Origin and Development of Classic and Contemporary "Word of Faith" Theologies* (Tulsa, OK: Word & Spirit Press,. 2008).

[7] Joe McIntyre, *E.W. Kenyon and His Message of Faith: the True Story*. 2010 edition (Bothell, WA: Empowering Grace Ministries, 1997, 2010).

[8] A. J. Gordon, *The Ministry of Healing: or The Miracle of Cure for All Ages*, ed. Third Edition - Revised (New York, NY: Fleming B. Revell, 1882).

[9] T. L. Osbom, *Healing the Sick* (Tulsa, OK: Harrison House, 1951,1977, 1981, 1986,1992).

[10] Herbert Benson, *Timeless Healing: The Biology of Belief* (New York, NY: A Fireside Book by Simon and Schuster, 1996,1997), 273.

CHAPTER SEVEN

The Classical Pentecostal Stream

Historically speaking I believe no movement has had a greater contribution to God's mighty river of healing than the Pentecostal Movement. When it began the Pentecostal Movement embraced the best teaching of the Faith Cure Movement, but it was different in that it saw itself as the fulfillment of the hope that had been expressed within Protestantism for almost a century. This hope was that right before the end of time and the coming of Jesus, He would once again pour out upon His Church a great empowering anointing. This anointing would include the restoration not only of the gifts of the Holy Spirit, but the Ephesians 4 offices of the apostle, prophet, evangelist, pastor and teacher. The "latter rain" of the Holy Spirit would be poured out on a Church that had been looking forward to a new Pentecost, to a recovery of apostolic Christianity. This restoration of apostolic Christianity that preceded the second coming of Jesus would include both "situational" and "constituted" gifts of the Holy Spirit for the people of God.

The Pentecostal Movement adopted the theology of the Faith Cure movement in regard to healing. The Word of Faith movement wouldn't be born for several years yet.

With the birth of Pentecostalism, the doctrine of divine healing experienced a renewal. In addition to the importance of one's own faith was the addition of hope and faith that you might receive a healing through someone who has the gift of healing or a special anointing for healing, most likely a healing evangelist. The teaching regarding healing in early Pentecostalism was similar to Faith Cure in that God would heal you when and if you "meet the conditions." "The conditions" primarily meant that you confess all sin and have faith.

Charles Price, a well-educated (Oxford University) Baptist, who was part of the early years of Pentecostalism's emphasis upon healing wrote a book called *Real Faith*, which emphasized the gift of faith. He understood the passage; "have faith *in* God" to actually be in the Greek, "have faith *of* God." This shifted the focus from "achieving" the conditions, which put the burden for healing on the sick person alone, to the evangelist and the sick person receiving the gift of the "faith of God." This was God's faith given to either or both that resulted in a healing. This kind of faith came most often to those whose minds were transformed by the teaching of the word of God.

Pentecostalism would birth most of the great healing evangelists of our time and would produce the greatest missionary expansion in the history of Protestantism. Today approximately 80% or more of all Christians in Latin America, Africa, and Asia have had Pentecostal experiences. This is not surprising since the baptism of the Holy Spirit was present for the power to witness.

Out of the great Healing Revival of 1948, with William Branham, Oral Roberts, Jack Coe, A.A. Allen, T.L. Osborn and many others, a new focus broke forth in the Church. The emphasis was now on the "anointed man of God, God's man of power for the hour." Faith and hope were tied in some way to the testimonies of how God was now sovereignly giving a restoration of the healing evangelist back to the Church.

There were other healing evangelists that predated Pentecostalism and were part of the earliest days of Pentecostalism. This 1948 revival was a reawakening of this gift and its role. Faith's focus was not solely based upon an ability to believe for healing, but faith could be augmented by the supernatural faith of, and anointing on the healing evangelists that God was restoring to the Church. The worship of thousands, and sometimes scores of thousands, that gathered at the healing tent as they sang "only believe, only believe, all things are possible, only believe," along with the testimonies of others who had been healed, created an atmosphere of faith and expectancy which was exactly the right environment for a miracle.

This faith was present because there was a sense that the sovereign timing of God. God had arisen. God had decreed that anything was possible if the evangelist could only get the people to believe with Him. Because belief existed that this was a sovereign visitation of God, God's healing revival, God's restoration of the New Testament type evangelist with strong gifts of healing, there was a new and heightened expectancy of faith for healing.

Multiple thousands were healed. So many healings began to take place that after a while people were no longer in awe. They began to take for granted what God was doing. The healings and miracles no longer evoked the kind of gratitude and praise they once had. This grieved the Holy Spirit and brought the Healing Revival to an end.[1] This along with the moral failure of some of the evangelists, and some of the inappropriate emphasis placed on monetary offerings contributed to the loss of faith and respect from the American public.

My great uncle was a Pentecostal preacher during this era. He had a child who was severely handicapped from birth. The child couldn't walk or talk; he was hydrocephalic and mentally handicapped. His father took him to the big tent meetings to be prayed for by Oral Roberts in hope of a healing but it never came. Still he preached a gospel that included healing though his own first-born was never healed.

What began by adopting the emphasis and theology of the Faith Cure Movement, that originated out of the Holiness Movement within the Evangelical denominations, especially those who had an emphasis upon entering into some kind of post conversion sanctification or Baptism of the Holy Spirit, gradually underwent changes. The emphasis moved away from the sick individual's faith in the promises of God appropriated through positive confession, to faith in the gift of healing that somehow was at work in a healing evangelist. Faith was still essential, but now personal faith was augmented by the faith of the healing evangelist.

Long before the 1948 Healing Revival, which resulted in scores of thousands of healings and millions of salvations, there had been evangelists with strong healing anointing. Alexander Dowie, Maria Woodworth-Etter, Smith Wigglesworth, and John G. Lake were among the first. Then in the 1920s and 1930s Aimee Semple-McPherson, F.F. Bosworth and Charles Price would join the company of "God's anointed" along with the Jeffrey brothers in England, and John Sung in China.[2]

Another outpouring of the Spirit that would result in major evangelistic healing crusades would be the 1947 Latter Rain Movement that was rejected by most Pentecostal denominations by 1949. Interestingly William Branham was instrumental in influencing both the Latter Rain and the 1948 Healing Revival. Branham had a visitation by an angel in 1946 who told him that God was going to release a great revival of healing and nothing would be able to resist the healing anointing, not even cancers, if William could get the people to believe.[3]

Branham would be anointed and gifted for this ministry. He was given a powerful word of knowledge gift that was used to bolster the faith of the people. He was the inspiration that caused others to seek God for this gift in prayer and fasting like Oral Roberts, and T.L. Osborn, and he was part of the inspiration that caused the leaders at Sharon Orphanage in Saskatchewan Canada to fast and pray for a visitation of God.[4] They did not have to wait long before the fire fell upon them.

Both the 1948 Healing Revival and the Latter Rain Movement had their own unique emphasis. The Latter Rain Movement had more of a focus on the local church, prophecy, spontaneous worship in tongues, and the restoration of all the office gifts, including the Prophet and Apostle.[5] Like Azusa Street before it, people would feel led of God to go to the nations. A great movement of God with the planting of churches would occur in Kenya resulting in thousands of churches being planted there after one of the "sent ones" heard God say after months of failure, "Go lay hands on the casket and command the person back to life." "The casket" was being carried on shoulders down the street of the city on the way to the graveyard. When the "sent one" obeyed there was a resurrection and revival began immediately.[6]

Another one who felt sent by God was Tommy Hicks who God used to break open the nation of Argentina through an unbelievable healing crusade that shook the nation.[7] Leaders from this move would train many of the present and last wave of revival leaders for the great waves of revival in Argentina.[8]

There were changes in the regular church services and their liturgies that would arise out of this move of God. Special services were added for healing. Churches began to work together to bring the "healing evangelist" to their communities, or a less famous healing evangelist to the local church. Pastors and leaders began to act like the famous healing evangelists, adopting both positive and negative influences. Anointing for healing with oil, taking handkerchiefs to the sick, and bringing the sick, even on stretchers, to special meetings for the desperate cases, would be added to the normal services. Though these practices existed in the earlier Pentecostal Movement, they were expanded during and after the 1947 Latter Rain Movement and the 1948 Healing Revival.

Like the Faith Cure movement, some of the early Pentecostal healing evangelists would develop "Healing Homes" where the desperate could come for prayer, or healing rooms like John G. Lake had in Spokane, Washington. Lake would also train up others for the ministry of healing, but this practice was not common. The more common practice focused on God's sovereign election or His calling of certain people into the office of healing evangelist.

The model for healing, influenced by the more flamboyant ministry of A. A. Allen, is an example of one such negative model for the local pastor. The Latter Rain Movement focused more on the local church and restoring the five-fold ministry to the local church than it did doing large citywide crusades. For the Latter Rain Movement the emphasis was not as much on the healing evangelist as it was on raising up people with the gifts of healing from within the local churches through the ministries of the prophets and apostles. The emphasis was more on the healing evangelists and crusades for those involved in the 1948 Healing Revival.

The Effect upon the Pastors and the Worship Service

How did the 1948 Healing Revival affect the role of the pastor? Pastors believed healing was in the atonement and would pray for healing, usually with their elders or the deacons in their church. They went to the hospitals to pray for healing for the sick from their churches, although there was not as much emphasis upon understanding what the Bible taught as was seen in the Faith Cure Movement and the Word of Faith Movement.

As the Latter Rain Movement began to impact the liturgy of the local church, prophetic ministry was recognized as valuable. People began singing in the spirit during worship, erupting in spontaneous praise, raising their hands, and believing that the gifts of healing should be expected to be given to people within the local church who would be released for the ministry of healing along with the pastor and his elders and deacons.

Local pastors were also impacted with a desire to become equippers of the laity. In order to facilitate this they would periodically have Prophetic Presbyteries, especially before setting people in places of service in the local church. Prophets were now not only giving words of encouragement; they would also often give directive words that had to be judged or evaluated by the pastor. If something seemed inaccurate, the pastor would be the one to bring balance to the prophetic gift by identifying and correcting the inaccuracy.

The pastors had a strong desire to move in the gifts of the spirit, especially the gift of prophecy, not unlike the Apostle Paul who saw and considered prophecy the highest gift. They would encourage their people to believe that the gifts of healing could be released to them, especially through the laying on of hands and a prophetic utterance from the presbytery (1 Timothy 4:14). The pastors in general evidenced biblical balance when it came to the gifts of the Holy Spirit.

endnotes

1   I was told this in a personal conversation with Pastor Tommy Tenney of Buffalo, NY who was pastor of a large Assembly of God church, and who as a young man worked with his father who was a healing evangelist with a traveling tent.

2   John Sung, *The Diaries of John Sung: An Autobiography*, Stephen L. Sheng, ed. (Brighton, MI: Stephen L. Sheng and Luke Sheng, 1995). Dr. John Sung was not a Pentecostal, but a holiness preacher who believed the evidence of the Baptism in the Holy Spirit "was the love of God and men," iv. He died in 1944 after 12 years of evangelistic ministry at 44 years of age.

3   D.E. Harrell, *All Things Are Possible: The Healing and Charismatic Revivals in Modern America* (Bloomington, IN: Indiana University Press, 1978), 25.

4   Allan Anderson, *An Introduction to Pentecostalism* (Cambridge University press, 2004) p. 58 Richard Riss, Latter Rain: The Latter Rain Movement of 1948 and the Mid-Twentieth Century Evangelical Awakening (Etobicoke, Ontario: Honeycomb Visual Productions Ltd., 1987).

5   Erskine Holt, interview by Randy Clark, (January 1995).

6   Randy Clark, interview with former President of Elim Bible Institute (I believe this was Paul Johansson).

7   Dr. R. Edward Miller, *Cry for Me Argentina* (Brentwood, Essex: Sharon Publications Ltd, 1988), 39-50.

8   Dr. Pablo Deiros and Dr. Carlos Mrarida, interview by Randy Clark, (1995).

the healing river

CHAPTER EIGHT

Equipping The Saints – The Third Wave Stream

The ministry of John Wimber and the Vineyard Movement, now known as the Association of Vineyard Churches, represents a stream which is sometimes called the Third Wave, a term given it by C. Peter Wagner. Wimber's exposure through the teaching opportunity with Wagner at Fuller Theological Seminary, and the popular Christian magazine that published the booklet MC510 that was sent to thousands of leaders describing what God was doing at Fuller, created a new move of the Spirit.

John Wimber became a Quaker pastor after accepting the Lord. When he asked for the blessing of his Quaker church to start a new church, a Calvary Chapel, he received it. This was later God's answer to John when the Spirit visited his church and people were shaking and falling.

Unlike the Pentecostal healing evangelist who saw a model of Branham and wanted to be like him, John did not like the model of healing he saw in Pentecostalism. Neither did he have an angel appear to him to commission him. He did not fast and pray for an anointing to heal as Oral Roberts had done. Instead, from his study of the Bible he felt impressed by the Holy Spirit that the Bible taught we were to pray for the sick. John had the impression to either begin praying for the sick or to "get out; out of the church, out of ministry, out of the Kingdom!"

As a result of this experience he began to invite people to come to the front of the church during Sunday evening services. I believe for seven months he invited the sick to come every Sunday night, and no one was healed. Still he persisted because he felt the Holy Spirit lead him to do so as a result of his study of the Bible. After seven long months the dam broke and healings began.

John and his spiritual sons would spread out around the world in the next four years with the message that "everybody gets to pray; just do it; we are to equip the saints for the work of the ministry." Throughout his ministry he encouraged everyone to "do the stuff." The emphasis was not on the constituted gift given to a healing evangelist, but instead it was on the situational gifting needed at the moment for anyone to minister to the person in front them who had a need. God could direct prayer by activating a word of knowledge or prophetic gift that could be received and used by any believer in Christ who had experienced regeneration.

There were no superstars in John's church. The equipped saints were now an army of prayers raised up and trained to recognize when God wanted them to do something. John taught that the church was not to be ashamed of what God did in our midst. He felt we weren't to hide this ministry. People needed to see God come and touch others.

Disagreement over this issue of the public ministry of healing and other types of ministry would result in Wimber being asked to leave the Calvary Chapel movement and join the Vineyard, which had seven churches at the time and was being led by Ken Gulliksen. Ken Gulliksen was the founder of the first Vineyard and instrumental in helping start the other six.

I joined the Vineyard Movement and became a leader in the early days, and I can tell you that John Wimber was an amazing man. He loved God, he honored Christ, he enjoyed fellowship with the Holy Spirit, and he wanted to experience everything the Bible says is possible.

I had opportunities to join several Pentecostal denominations after the powerful seminar at my Baptist church, but I felt God was leading me into the Vineyard. I liked the Vineyard theology regarding healing and its strong emphasis on learning how to move naturally in the super-natural. I felt that the Vineyard was on the cutting edge of what God was doing. It was a place to go and fit in if you were an evangelical who had been filled with the Holy Spirit, and who embraced all the gifts of the Holy Spirit as still for today.

If you wanted to be involved in healing the sick, casting out demons, ministering to the poor and planting churches the Vineyard was the place to do it. In the Vineyard there was great allowance for doctrinal diversity and there was John. It was near impossible not to love him. He seemed so different, so non-religious, so genuine, so humble, yet so confident in God.

In the Vineyard one could embrace all the gifts, the signs and won-ders, healing and miracles, but you did not have to believe that tongues were the necessary initial evidence of the Holy Spirit's baptism. There was a strong emphasis upon the value of tongues and the utility of the gift, and at one point there were more people in the Vineyard, percentage wise, speaking in tongues, than in some Pentecostal denominations.

I loved all of it. I loved being a third wave evangelical as we called ourselves. It was not enough for a pastor to teach or preach about the Kingdom; the Vineyard pastor needed and desired to demonstrate the power of the Kingdom of God. This was no safe place for the timid of heart. As John Wimber would so often say, "Faith is spelled, RISK." My eighteen years in the Vineyard, from 1984 to 2001, were productive times of growth, challenge and maturing. For the first time in my life enough healings were occurring that I could say that healing had become normative. It was no longer the exception.

Today there remain spiritual sons of John Wimber who continue to take his message to the nations, to pastors, and to the laity, and who try to model less flamboyant ways of ministering. They are not looking for a new "healing evangelist" who will minster to scores of thousands. Instead they are looking to release scores of thousands of "little ole me's" who will take this healing ministry into scores of thousands of communities, and into the workplace, and into homes; "little ole me's" who believe God can use them.

These spiritual sons of Wimber feel the more extravagant models of ministry to be too awkward for them so by design they try to offer a low hype, low emotion, low key, but high anointing way to engage people for healing. A Wimberism for this model for ministry is teaching people how to "naturally move in the supernatural, without hype or manipulation." I personally want to cheer on old friends in the Vineyard like Steve Nicholson in Evanston, Illinois and Bill Jackson in the San Diego area, Mike Hudgins in Laguna Niguel, California, and Happy Leman in Urbana, Illinois. May God use you to raise up many sons and daughter to keep the dream alive; the dream that we all can pray - that we're all called to "do the stuff."

Not only does John Wimber have sons in the Vineyard, he has sons outside the Vineyard as well; sons who were influenced through his teachings on the message of the Kingdom as he modeled "doing it" and not just talking about it. There are people outside the Vineyard like Bill Johnson who I believe carries John's teaching anointing about the Kingdom. Bill is raising up sons and daughters spiritually to believe the message that the Kingdom of God is at hand and then sending them out to this nation and the nations of the world. Bill, like John Wimber, is giving away the ministry to others and asking others to have their minds transformed by the renewing of the Word.

Others like Che Ahn, John Arnott, Rolland and Heidi Baker and I believe in the message of the Kingdom, and like Wimber try to naturally minister in the supernatural. We believe that little ole me's can be used mightily. We believe that poor people with little or no formal education can be used to raise the dead in places like Mozambique. We see an army of sons and daughters being raised up who believe that the words of Jesus are true:

I tell you the truth, anyone who has faith in me will do what I have been doing. He will do even greater things than these, because I am going to the Father.

(John 14:12 NIV)

Together we want to keep the dream alive. We believe that to make a disciple is to equip someone to not only know and live the teachings and values of Jesus, but to disciple them to heal the sick and cast out demons so that they are able to tell people, "The Kingdom of God is at hand; start thinking differently about what is possible in life!"

I loved this season of my life, and for eighteen years I continued within the Vineyard Movement. Even though I eventually left the Vineyard I have tried to remain true to the essential values that I saw in John Wimber and learned in the Vineyard from him. I love the emphasis that healing is learning how to co-labor with Jesus; that we are not able to do anything in ourselves, but only what we saw the Father doing. To this day I still do not like to see healing claims exaggerated or hyped. I do not like manipulation, pride, or bragging. I still believe in everything John Wimber taught me, but I believe in more than he taught me. My pursuit of more anointing led me out of the Baptist denomination and in 1993 led me to look outside the Vineyard Movement.

A friend who had experienced the outpouring in my Baptist church nine years earlier called me and told me about an evangelist, Rodney Howard-Browne, from South Africa, who was being used by God to bring refreshing and joy to burned-out Christians. I certainly qualified. He told me about the bizarre phenomena that occurred in Howard-Browne's meetings, and most importantly he told me that Rodney had said God had told him, "You will lay your hands on one thousand pastors who will receive the anointing on your life and will help you take revival all over the world."

I wanted to be one of the thousand. I asked my friend what the fruit of his experience had been after receiving prayer from Rodney Howard-Browne. He responded, "I have seen more people healed in the past two weeks since I returned from Rodney's meetings than I have seen in the past eight years." God really knew how to hook me, how to catch my attention and create a new hunger for Him in my soul. I went and I received! God did exceedingly above what I had asked or imagined.

Within a few months word was out about the powerful impartation on Randy Clark from Rodney Howard-Brown. The power of the Holy

Spirit was falling in my church, and it fell at the annual Midwest Region-al Vineyard Pastors Conference too, resulting not only in people being refreshed in a very powerful manner, but in many healings. News of all of this opened the door for me to go to the Airport Vineyard Church in Toronto for what was supposed to be a four-day meeting. I went and God showed up in great power and the people came.

My very first night in Toronto a woman was healed of a terminal ill-ness. The healings and miracles continued. People streamed to Toronto from all over the world. The meetings that were originally to have lasted four nights continued six nights a week for the next twelve and a half years. They became known as the Toronto Blessing and were the longest protracted meetings in the history of North America.

One of the strengths of the Vineyard Church that emerged in Toronto was the New Testament model of equipping the saints for the work of the ministry (Ephesians 4:11-12). Gone was the Old Testament model, the one-man show. The new model that emerged was dependent upon trained lay people to assist the leadership in the ministry of healing.

The Airport Vineyard became Airport Christian Fellowship (TACF) [now known as Catch the Fire Toronto] and had one of the best-trained teams for ministry that I had ever seen. This emphasis upon lay ministry was consistent with the heart and vision of John Wimber. John and Carol Arnott, the pastors of the church in Toronto, did an excellent job of preparing their church for a visitation of the Holy Spirit, lead-ing it during a long season of revival and developing a multi-campus church that today is overseen by other pastors at their many campuses.

Effect on Pastors and Worship Services

The Vineyard is an example of a third-wave church. Three of the six leaders of the Revival Alliance were involved in the Vineyard move-ment, and the other three were impacted by it.

As one of the six leaders of the Revival Alliance I believe there is a strong third-wave influence upon several of the leaders. Our understanding of the gifts, particularly the gifts of word of knowledge, prophecy, and gifts of healing require the pastors to press in for more anointing for healing, more understanding of healing, and more ability to move in the gifts that are often associated with healing, especially words of knowledge.

Pastors within the six networks that make up the Revival Alliance need to develop, by practice, a greater sensitivity and accuracy in the operation of the gifts; of the gift of word of knowledge and of the gift of prophecy. These gifts have a connection to healing, especially inner healing. The pastors need to seek out understanding of the ways of God in relation to the ministry of healing. They need to grow in their understanding of the Kingdom of God and to discover how to operate in the gift of faith, working with the Holy Spirit to create an environment that is more conducive for faith to occur in the people of their congregation.

This third-wave influence has also had an effect upon the order of service, the liturgy of the church. It places a higher value on worship because it is believed that breakthroughs come and spontaneous healings begin to occur when we enter His glory realm through worship. Not only do we expect breakthroughs in healing during worship, but we are open to God breaking in and breaking through and taking us into spontaneous worship, and to His new songs.

I will never forget the time I awoke from a deep sleep to God's strong internal voice saying, "When my presence is in your midst in worship, so is my power to heal." This occurred the Monday after a powerful worship service. Up until this time I had not made a strong enough connection between God's presence during worship and the presence of His power for healing.

Several years later this insight would cause a great breakthrough in the way in which I ministered during church services. On occasion I would be prompted by the Spirit to declare to the congregation that "God was going to heal during the following song." We would sing the song, entering into glorious worship, and then, at the conclusion of the song, we would count to three and shout. The people would then inspect their bodies to see if healing had occurred. I have seen hundreds healed in this way in one meeting, thousands healed in this manner in another meeting, and more often scores healed through the declaration of sensing God giving me the liberty to make the declaration. These declarations are not common, perhaps one in every 100 meetings.

The influence of third-wave theology would bring about a shift that valued training the laity for ministering in the Spirit. No longer was it up to the pastor alone. In addition, prophetic evangelism and mercy ministries among the poor, including healing, emerged along with openness to the Holy Spirit to speak in congregational meetings especially through prophetic words.

This new wave of participatory worship ushered in an era in which the congregation was invited to enter into the experience of the presence of God and as a result experience healing as well as the gifts of the Spirit.

the healing river

PART THREE

Where Do We Go From Here

CHAPTER NINE

Let The River Flow

There is so much mystery to healing. No one truly has all the answers to all the theological, scientific and medical questions that arise around healing. Why is there such inconsistency or such an uncontrollable element experienced by those who have healing ministries? Why isn't everyone healed? Why do we sometimes see the first up get healed and then no more? Why is it that oftentimes no one is healed for an hour and then everyone left gets healed? Why does the "glory cloud" sometimes appear and people are sovereignly healed without being prayed for? These and so many other questions beg answers.

We want to understand more regarding our "why" questions, but we also want to understand more about the "how" aspect of healing. How does healing happen in our bodies; how does cancer die when cursed in Jesus' name? How do tumors sometimes instantly disappear? How are the effects of Parkinson's disease reversed in a matter of minutes or a few hours? How are people born blind given sight or those born deaf given hearing? How are stroke victims restored? How are chromosomes rewritten? And mystery of all mysteries - how is a person who has been dead for four hours, who has experienced total oxygen deprivation, raised from the dead through prayer? Not only raised from the dead, but without any brain damage. There is so much for us to learn and to understand about healing. We want to know what is happening when people are being healed, yet healing remains in the realm of mystery.

I do not think it will be easy to discover the answers to our questions through medical science because the scientific method must be reproducible. Medical science has not yet developed technology that is capable of explaining what is happening or why some phenomena in the human body happen when a person is healed. I believe that the best machine, the best technology for recording what is happening in the human body is the human body itself, and the soul.

Even when the person receiving healing can explain what they are feeling, it remains a mystery as to why they are feeling these sensations, and an even greater mystery is what is causing these sensations or phenomena. Many people feel heat as they are being healed, with some experiencing tremendous heat immediately prior to their healing. Oftentimes this heat will remain for several hours or even all night upon the area of the body that needs healing. Others feel electricity coursing through their bodies as they are being healed.[1] There are a large percentage of people who are healed who have no sense of anything physical before their healing.[2] Sometimes I think this percentage who feel nothing might be as high as fifty percent of those healed in a particular meeting Other times, I think the percentage might be closer to forty percent of those healed who feel nothing with sixty percent feeling the heat, energy, tingling, cold, wind, or other phenomena prior to the healing.

It is becoming increasingly obvious that faith plays an extremely important role in healing but what exactly is its role? Medical science is finding evidence that faith does have an effect upon our bodies, and often does bring healing, yet we do not know what exactly causes the effect of faith. I am not speaking here of divine healing, but merely faith healing; faith in the doctor, faith in the procedure, and faith in medicine, all of which can produce healing. Medical evidence abounds to give credence to this faith element. It is called the "placebo effect".[3] There is also a "nocebo effect" that can cause a person who is healthy to die for no apparent medical reason.[4] There can be faith healing that is not divine healing, and there can be divine healing that is not faith healing, but the most common experience for those of us in the Church and the Kingdom of God is to see divine healing as a result of faith.

Could it be that God has created us to be people of faith, to accomplish what seems to be miraculous by or through faith, and of whom it is said, *"Without faith it is impossible to please God."* (Hebrews 11:6 NIV) Could it be that God has hard-wired our bodies to respond to faith, and if so, isn't the good news of grace instead of Karma an excellent basis for faith?[5]

God has gone to extremes to create faith in us. He gives us the Holy Spirit who gives the gift of faith. He gives His word in the Bible with its tremendous, almost unbelievable promises to encourage our faith and to be the basis for our faith. He gives us promises about healing, and about miracles, and about authority granted to us in Jesus' name. He tells us that all things are possible; that we can command the mountains to move into the sea, and have what we ask if we do not doubt. On top of all this, He anchors these promises in the Covenant, through the sacrificial death of Jesus who bore our sicknesses and diseases in His body when he was crucified, just as he bore our sins, trespasses, and iniquity (Isaiah 53). The New Testament is the revelation of a compassionate God who has come to destroy the works of the devil which includes sickness, disease, and spiritual oppression, depression, and bondage of the will.

I believe the human body was designed by its creator to respond to faith. I believe the human body has been created in such a way as to be impacted by faith. I believe God designed us this way because faith is so important to Him. Though our bodies respond to faith in medicine, and faith in doctors, and faith in procedures, this kind of faith is not the kind of faith that produces the miraculous, the greater things, the immediate cures, or the resurrections. When it comes to physical healing and deliverance, there is an historical difference in quality and quantity regarding healing between Christianity and other religious systems or non-religious systems.

There is within Christianity a rich history of healing. In the first three centuries of its existence the Church experienced a flood of healings and miracles that would not be surpassed again until the twentieth century which saw more healings and miracles than even the first three centuries. In the last decade of the twentieth century and the first twelve years of the twenty-first century the Church has seen more people raised from the dead than any other time in its history.[7] In fact, in every century during the past two thousand years the Church has reports of healings somewhere from within.

During the first three centuries after Jesus was crucified, raised from the dead, and taken into heaven, Christianity won over the gods of the Greco-Roman Empire of which there were many, primarily because of its greater power to heal and deliver people who were troubled by demons.[8] This power was the evidence of the power in Jesus' name that came through the outpouring of the Holy Spirit. This was a major reason Jesus came to die; to pour out this dispensation of grace. Grace is not just the undeserved mercy and forgiveness of God, but it is also the empowering energy or power of God which surpasses all other powers.

The experiences of the Apostle Paul in Ephesus give witness to this greater power of God to surpass all other powers. Acts 19:8-20 tells the story of how Paul brought the gospel into the city. Ephesus was a port city at the intersection of several major trade routes in western Asia Minor (now Turkey). It was also the intersection of many cultural beliefs. There was the Pagan worship of the Roman goddess Diana, the Jewish worship of God, and the Christian worship of the God of the Jews through Jesus Christ His Son. Many who first became Christians continued to adhere to pagan practices also.

In the midst of the geological transfer of the gospel that took place as Paul and the disciples brought the message to the whole Roman Empire, a spiritual transaction ensued as Jew and Gentile alike abandoned their beliefs when faced with the greater power of God in Jesus Christ His Son.

In Acts 19 verse 8, we see that even though Paul boldly preaches the gospel with persuasive arguments about the kingdom of God many remain obstinate and refuse to believe. It is only when God begins to do extraordinary miracles through Paul that people begin to take notice.

God did extraordinary miracles through Paul, so that even hand-
kerchiefs and aprons that had touched him were taken to the sick, and
their illnesses were cured and the evil spirits left them.

Some Jews who went around driving out evil spirits tired to invoke
the name of the Lord Jesus over those who were demon-possessed.
They would say, 'In the name of Jesus, whom Paul preaches, I com-
mand you to come out.' Seven sons of Sceva, a Jewish chief priest,
were doing this. One day, the evil spirit answered them, 'Jesus I know,
and I know about Paul, but who are you?' Then the man who had the
evil spirit jumped on them and overpowered them all. He gave them
such a beating that they ran out of the house naked and bleeding.

When this became known to the Jews and Greeks living in Ephesus,
they were all seized with fear, and the name of the Lord Jesus was
held in high honor. Many of those who believed now came and openly
confessed their evil deeds. A number who had practiced sorcery brought
their scrolls together and burned them publicly. When they calculated
the value of the scrolls, the total came to fifty thousand drachmas. In
this way the word of the Lord spread widely and grew in power.

(Acts 19:11-20 NIV)

The greater power of the name of Jesus as seen in Paul and the
disciples and other Christians brought about a revival of consecration
to God, as many forsook the trappings and teachings of paganism to
embrace Christianity.

Luke, the author of Acts, does not present a picture where only
apostles are involved in the ministry of healing, signs, and wonders, and
miracles or prophecy. He shows us in chapter 6, with the appointing of
the seven (who have been considered by some the first deacons) that others, not just apostles, moved in these powers from God. These seven that
were appointed seem more like evangelists than deacons to me. Philip is
called an evangelist, and Stephen is seen leading people to Christ with
wonders and miraculous signs; Acts 6:8 *"Now Stephen, a man full of*
God's grace and power, did great wonders and miraculous signs among

the people." (NIV) Again, in Acts 9 a disciple named Ananias is used to prophecy and brings healing to Saul, a persecutor of the Church, who would later become its greatest apostolic evangelist.

Luke also shows us that those who first took the gospel to the Gentiles were unknown lay people who fled Jerusalem during the persecution associated with Stephen's martyrdom. Unlike Peter's efforts where the Gentiles were god-fearers attached to the Jewish synagogue, these in Antioch were not. Who were these non-apostles and how did they, these men who have no names or titles or offices, successfully evangelize? We see in Acts 11:19 that it was men from Cyprus and Cyrene who evangelized Antioch. They were the first to go to the Greeks also.

> *Now those who had been scattered by the persecution in connection with Stephen traveled as far as Phoenicia, Cyprus and Antioch, telling the message only to Jews. Some of them, however, men from Cyprus and Cyrene, went to Antioch and began to speak to Greeks also, telling them the good news about the Lord Jesus. The Lord's hand was with them, and a great number of people believed and turned to the Lord.*
>
> (Acts 11:19-21 NIV)

How did they do it? How did they evangelize? They shared the good news about the Lord Jesus. If you look at the descriptions of the gospel in Acts, it is the gospel of the Kingdom of God that has come in Jesus. In Him a power has been released to help believers/followers/disciples with their problems, including healing and deliverance. This is the gospel of the Kingdom in Jesus.

Verse twenty-one gives further insight into how God used them. "The Lord's hand was with them" is a Hebraism for the power of God being with them. The Lord's hand was often used to describe his power. What did this result in? Verse twenty-one gives us the answer in a context that is surely meant to be understood as causal, "and a great number of people believed and turned to the Lord." This is how the gospel reached Antioch.

In Antioch a church would be formed that would become a great missionary church. Its power for advancing the gospel to other cities in Asia Minor was that it had people who heard from God through prophecies, visions, and dreams. These people, these teachers and prophets, would be sent out at the Lord's direction and would come back transformed into apostles by their experiences of persecution, imprisonment, stoning, shipwreck, and suffering. This is what happened to Barnabas and Saul. This team of prophet and teacher came back Paul and Barnabas, both apostles. Yet, we must remember that this great missionary church wasn't established through the work of apostles, but through ordinary lay people who also had the power of God upon them and through God worked so powerfully that the phrase, "the Lord's hand was with them" became reality as "a great number of people believed and turned to the Lord." I believe in context and based upon the Hebrew Old Testament this was a reference to the signs and wonders, the healings, miracles, and deliverances.

This is what the Church of God, the Church of our Lord Jesus Christ needs today. She needs the restoration of the early gifts, all of Her gifts, upon all the different streams that comprise the Church; not just the Pentecostal and Charismatic denominations, but also the Protestants, the Roman Catholic Church, and the Orthodox Church.

It is this understanding of the Kingdom that I am wrestling for, against years of tradition and new theology that changed the makeup of the Church; wrestling against the traditions of men and women (but honestly the men are the ones who messed up the Church's self-understanding). This wrestling today is to awaken a Church that in the Westernized world is partially asleep. May the gospel of the Kingdom be restored to its fullness; not just a gospel of forgiveness, but a gospel of empowerment as well. May our methods of evangelism no longer be limited to debate and argument, but may they be augmented by his gracelets of healing and working of miracles.

It is in this light that we must hear again the gospel of Matthew's recording of Jesus' Great Commission.

*"Then Jesus came to them and said, "All authority in heaven and on earth
has been given to me. 19 Therefore go and make disciples of all nations,
baptizing them in the name of the Father and of the Son and of the Holy
Spirit, 20 and teaching them to* **obey everything I have commanded
you.** *And surely I am with you always, to the very end of the age."*

(Matthew 28:18-20 NIV)

We must teach the disciples not only when to be baptized (and
usually today this baptism follows teaching on the doctrine of the Faith).
We must teach the new disciples to also do what Jesus commanded the
twelve and the seventy to do when they were commissioned. Discipleship in the first century was not merely learning the teachings of the
master discipler, but also learning to model their lives on his life, believing like he did, behaving like he did, and doing what he did.

If you are a Christian you probably recognize the Matthew 28:18
passage as the "Great Commission." We are not only to go and make
disciples, but we are to teach the disciples to obey (do) everything Jesus
commanded the twelve disciples to do. This is discipleship; not just
studying the Bible, or learning principles to live by, but also doing what
the master [Jesus] modeled for us to do. Jesus commanded the seventy to
do what he commanded the twelve to do.

My professor of theology for my doctoral program taught that we are
to understand the Great Commission in light of these two commissions
– learn the biblical principles for living and do what Jesus did. The
commands of healing and deliverance top the list of the commandments
of Jesus and are connected to the announcement of the Good News of the
Kingdom of God having been inaugurated in the coming of Jesus.

There is a Christian leader today who is accusing Pentecostals and
Charismatics of having "strange fire on the altar" which he thinks is a
reference to ungodly practices when in fact it is a reference to the gifts
of the Spirit. I don't believe we need to be concerned with strange fire as
much as we need to be concerned with teaching that has little support
from Scripture for its application. Or teaching that has some scriptural

support but lacks the necessary tension with other scriptures of the Bible to keep a healthy balance in a life of faith.

It is not "strange fire" I fear for the church. It is the alternative of almost no fire, no charismata, no signs and wonders and no miracles, which indicates to me either no fire or very little fire. The problem is that the "fire of God" isn't connected primarily to perfect doctrine, but more to personal relationship with Jesus by simple childlike faith. It is the belief that the miracles were given to authenticate correct doctrine rather than to accompany the announcement of the good news of the in break of God's powerful Kingdom that has caused much division within the Church.

The real "strange fire" we need to be concerned about is the fire connected to power worked by the occult, by demonic entities, and by people who have an antichrist spirit. This antichrist spirit is one that denies that Jesus came in the flesh, that God became incarnate in Jesus who is the "only" begotten Son of God. This is the teaching of New Age as seen in Theosophy and energy healing modalities such as Reiki, Therapeutic Touch, and Healing Touch.

There is today a great need to have true discernment between real fire and strange fire from God. Wesley understood that wherever God's real fire is manifested the enemy will try to bring wild fire. Wesley's use of wild fire means the same as the present day use of strange fire. What Wesley feared more than wild fire was the church not having the fire of God.

An empowered laity was evangelizing Antioch while most of the apostles were still in Jerusalem. Later, the Apostles would "get it" and would follow the examples of the laity in Antioch. Just as those in the early church who went to the Greeks were called, I am calling you to join the army of little ole me(s) who are a people who love Jesus, trust his Father, have fellowship with His Holy Spirit, and who hear from Him and obey His instructions. This is the army who can experience the awesome Hebraism, "The Lord's hand was upon them."

I want the reality of the Lord's hand upon me – don't you? I know there should be a correlation between his presence and his power. I know there is a definite relationship between faith and miracles and healings, and I know there is a definite relationship between faith and receiving revelation from God about what he wants to do. Jesus said His sheep would hear his voice (John 10:3, 4; 27). He promised revelation from heaven that would lead us as it did the men from Cyprus and Cyrene. When you understand the way He communicates His will for specific situations of healing and miracles, and deliverance and acts of mercy or justice, you will experience faith and you will experience "the Lord's hand being with you!"

I believe we, the Church, no longer have the option to argue if healing is for today because the majority of the world's cultures believe it is and will find it in the occult or other religions if it is not offered by the Church.

It is time for all Christians to wake up to the real spiritual and ideological battle. Not between Pentecostals and Protestants, not between Catholics and Charismatics, not between Christians and Christians. That was the battle of the 19th and 20th centuries. WAKE UP CHURCH! The 21st century battle is the battle between Jesus Christ and the god of healing in the New Age movement. Paul, in his letter to the Ephesians says,

Awake, O sleeper, and arise from the dead, and Christ will shine on you. Look carefully then how you walk, not as unwise but as wise, making the best use of the time, because the days are evil. Therefore do not be foolish, but understand what the will of the Lord is.

(Ephesians 5:14b-15 ESV)

Aesclepius, the last of the pagan gods of Europe to have his temples re-consecrated as churches, because he had the greatest allegiance upon the minds and hearts of the pagans, seems to have risen to challenge the Church. Ironically, the Church defeated him through greater healings, more healings, and greater and more deliverances in Jesus' name than were happening in the name of Aesclepius'. With the doctrine of Cessationism and the theological perspective of liberalism Aesclepius finds a different gospel in much of the Church than he did in the first century.

I do not mean that I believe in the literal reincarnation or resurrection of a man named Aesclepius, but rather the demonic power behind the worship in the Aeslepian temples. It is this alternative healer who is drawing greater allegiance every day while the Church in North America and Western Europe is, to a great degree, stuck in Cessationism and liberalism.

God is still after the nations. He is interested in revival regardless of denomination. I believe that the coming revival is going to be big, so much bigger than we can imagine because what God is after is so much bigger than our thinking. His Spirit is going to bring unity; an ecumenism of the Spirit rather than doctrinal ecumenicism. We will be able to recognize our brothers and sisters in Christ because of the Spirit of Jesus in them; the same Holy Spirit that is at work in us will be at work in them.

I believe this coming move of God will be so big that we will need all of the churches, across denominational lines, to reap the harvest, the millions that are going to come into His kingdom. We are going to need His presence and His power because apart from signs and wonders and the gifts of the Holy Spirit, many more of those who don't know Him will not be awakened to His truth. When we allow God's miracles and signs and wonders into the Church, we bring glory to God.

If the Church will take seriously the gifts of the Holy Spirit and the ministry of healing, we will find ourselves in a place where the heavens open and the power of evil is confronted and limited; the gifts will come forth and we will see healings, and the lost will be saved. He tells us in His word that *"the earth will be filled with the knowledge of the glory of the Lord, as the waters cover the sea."* (Habakkuk 2:14 NIV) The Church must awaken to the knowledge that God's great power to heal is available for us today if we will only move beyond the doctrinal differences that have become impediments to the flow of His mighty river of healing and let the floodgates of heaven open and the King of Glory come in!

endnotes

1   youtube/mukaOJJJbtQ

2   For example Mike Gibson, who was a member of my Executive Director's church in Engle-wood, Florida was in hospice. He had only a few weeks to live. He was a hemophiliac and had contracted AIDS during a blood transfusion. His wife persuaded him to come to the meeting. He was in a wheelchair and had a patch over one eye to prevent his double vision. I prayed for him. He felt nothing, and there was no indication of improvement after the time of prayer. Nothing changed for the next two days, but on the third morning he woke up feeling stronger. He continued improving every day. He was completely healed of AIDS, had more children, and lived another twelve years. When he fell into sin the AIDS returned after 12 years. Once again he came to me for prayer, I prayed for his healing, but this time he wasn't healed and died in a couple of years. In Goiania, Brazil a man who had muriatic acid spilled in his eyes as a small boy was healed after 50 plus years of complete blindness. When you looked into his eyes all you could see was white scar tissue over the pupils and corneas. A woman on my team prayed for him for five hours in one night. He felt nothing. There was no change. She felt nothing, only the strong conviction to continue praying though there were none of the normal signs of the healing presence of Jesus, heat and/or energy. When the woman left for America the next day she felt discouraged. There were six blind persons healed in the meeting, but not the man she prayed for. Three days later the pastor of the Videra Church called me and told me it was the greatest miracle in the his-tory of the city. This man had awakened on the third morning after prayer with no scar tissue and new pupils and corneas. The doctors had him return to the hospital three times, each time asking him, "Tell us again, how is it you can see?"

3   Herbert Benson, "Chapter 9 Wired for God," in *Timeless Healing: The Power and Biology of Belief*, 195-217 (New York, NY: A Fireside Book by Simon and Schuster, 1996, 1997), 21, 24, 27.

4   Benson, *Timeless Healing*, 49.

5   A major block I have seen for people to receive healing is a sense that they deserve their health problem due to their lifestyle (diet, lack of sleep, lack of exercise, etc.), or their immorality (PTSDs due to sexual immorality or a sense of guilt for some other type of failure), or a self hatred often connected to the treatment by others (causing psychosomatic illnesses), or their inability to release others who have wronged them by forgiveness resulting in bitterness (this causes many kinds of illnesses). In all these ways people believe they have caused their illness or at least deserve their illness. It is difficult to see them healed if they believe they are getting what they deserve, a strong element of the doctrine of Karma. However, if they can believe in and accept grace then the way is cleared theologically, emotionally, spiritually, to be much more open to faith for their healing.

6   I believe an explanation for this was the early Church understood the death, resurrection, ascension, and pouring out of the Holy Spirit, the heart of the gospel resulted in the Church receiving power of disease, demons, and death. Theologically this is called the *Christus Victor* understanding of the atonement. Jesus Christ is victor over these things. However, later the gospel was truncated to not be focused so much on present needs, but on future life in heaven. The em-phasis moved from the supernatural power to heal, deliver, even raise the dead, to the emphasis on being forgiven and going to heaven. Theologically this view is called the *Substitutionary Atone-ment*. The earlier view, *Christus Victor* did include the understanding of forgiveness and going to heaven or having eternal life, but it had a much more powerful emphasis upon God's power to help with the problems of life in this life. Only since about 1900 did this earlier understanding of the gospel begin to be restored to the church. During the last fifty years the Christus Victor view has been reintroduced by rediscovering the message of the gospel as the message of the inbreak-ing of the power of the Kingdom of God upon the earth with the coming of Jesus. Gustaf Aulen, *Christus Victor: An Historical Study of the Three Main Types of the Idea of Atonement*, trans. H. G. Herbert (New York, NY: MacMillan Publishing Co., 1969). George Eldon Ladd, *The Kingdom of God* (Carlisle: Paternoster Press, 1959).

[7] Dr. Craig Keener writes of hundreds of these dead raisings in his book *Miracles*. Keener, Craig S., *Miracles: The Credibility of the New Testament Accounts* , 2 vols. (Grand Rapids, Michigan: Baker Academic, 2011), 730-760. Craig S. Keener, *Studies of Extraordinary Claims in Non-Christian Movements*, Vol 1, in *Miracles: The Credibility of the New Testament Accounts*. 242-249 (Grand Rapids, MI: Baker Academic a division of Baker Publishing Co., 2011). I have met several of the families who had a member raised from the dead in Mozambique through the ministry of Iris Ministries led by Rolland and Heidi Baker. As of 2013 in less than 17 years they experienced over 450 dead raisings. This resulted in two whole provinces of northern Mozambique that were Muslim with almost no Christian population to experience such a turning to Jesus Christ that today the government lists those provinces as Christian. Several Americans who are related to our ministry as lay persons, not clergy, have been used to raise their children or grandchildren. And, recently in Brazil (2012) we met two children who had been raised from the dead, one of whom was in the hospital, brain dead, on life support. The mother brought a picture to the meeting. We prayed over the picture and the child came back to life before the mother returned to the hospital.

[8] Ramsay MacMullen, *Christianizing The Roman Empire A.D. 100-400* (New Haven, Connecticut: Yale University Press), 1984.

Bibliography

Anderson, Allan. *An Introduction to Pentecostalism.* Cambridge University press, 2004. Richard Riss, *Latter Rain: The Latter Rain Movement of 1948 and the Mid-Twentieth Century Evangelical Awakening* Etobicoke, Ontario: Honeycomb Visual Productions Ltd., 1987.

Benson, Herbert. *Timeless Healing: The Biology of Belief.* New York, NY: A Fireside Book by Simon and Schuster, 1996, 1997.

-----, Chapter 9 Wired for God, *Timeless Healing: The Power and Biology of Belief,* 195-217. New York, NY: A Fireside Book by Simon and Schuster, 1996, 1997.

Clark, Randy. The Relation of the Problem of Miracle to the New Testament Interpretation and Christian Faith, *A Paper Submitted to Dr. John Polhill of the Department of New Testament Interpretation Southern Baptist Theological Seminary in partial fulfillment for the requirement for Course N.T. S 33H "A study on the book of Acts"* (Louisville, KY, January 28, 1977).

------, Empowered: A School of Healing and Impartation, Published by Global Awakening.

------, *Unbelieving Believers and Believing Unbelievers*, in *The Essential Guide to Healing: Equipping All Christians to Pray for the Sick,* 87-110. Grand Rapids, MI: Chosen Books, 2011.

Culpepper, Robert. *An Evaluation of the Charismatic Movement: A Theological and Biblical Appraisal.* Valley Forge, PA: Judson Press, 1977.

Deiros, Dr. Pablo and Dr. Carlos Mrarida, interview by Randy Clark, 1995.

Green, Michael. *Evangelism in the Early Church.* Grand Rapids, Michigan: William B. Eerdmans Publishing Company, 1970.

Gordon, A. J. *The Ministry of Healing: or The Miracle of Cure for All Ages,* ed. Third Edition – Revised. New York, NY: Fleming B. Revell, 1882.

Harrell, D.E. *All Things Are Possible: The Healing and Charismatic Revivals in Modern America.* Bloomington, IN: Indiana University Press, 1978.

Harvey, Van A. *The Historian and the Believer: The Morality of Historical Knowledge and Christian Belief.* New York, New York: The MacMillan Company, 1966, 1996.

Holt, Erskine. Interview by Randy Clark, 1995.

Hyatt, Eddie L. *2000 Years of Charismatic Christianity.* Lake May, FL: Charisma House, 2002.

Kelsey, Morton. *Healing and Christianity.* San Francisco, CA: Harper and Row Publishers reprinted Augsburg Fortress, 1973, 1995. Augsburg Fortress Edition.

King, Paul L. *Only Believe: Examining the Origin and Development of Classic and Contemporary "Word of Faith" Theologies.* Tulsa, Oklahoma: Word & Spirit Press, 2008.

Luther, Martin. *A Mighty Fortress Is Our God.* 1529.

MacMullen, Ramsay. *Christianizing The Roman Empire A.D. 100-400.* New Haven, Connecticut: Yale University Press, 1984.

MacNutt, Francis. *Healing.* Notre Dame, IN: Ave Maria Press, 1974.

McConnell, D. R. *A Different Gospel: Biblical and Historical Insights into the Word of Faith Movement.* Peabody, MA: Hendrickson Publishers, 1995.

McGee, Gary B., Patrick H. Alexander and Stanley M. Burgess, ed. *Dictionary of Pentecostal and Charismatic Movements,* ed. Gary B. McGee, and Patrick H. Alexander Stanley M. Burgess. Grand Rapids, MI: Zondervan, 1988.

McIntyre, Joe. *E. W. Kenyon and His Message of Faith: the True Story.* 2010 edition. Bothell, WA: Empowering Grace Ministries, 1997, 2010.

Miller, Dr. R. Edward. *Cry for Me Argentina.* Brentwood, Essex: Sharon Publications Ltd, 1988.

Osborn, T. L. *Healing the Sick.* Tulsa, OK: Harrison House, 1951,1977, 1981, 1986,1992.

Pearson, Mark. *Christian Healing: A Comprehensive and Practical Guide.* Lake Mary, FL: Charisma House, 2004.

Ruthven, Jon. *On the Cessation of the Charismata: The Protestant Polemic on Post-Biblical Miracles,* Revised and Expanded Edition. Tulsa, OK: Word and Spirit Press, 1993, 2011.

------, *What's Wrong With Protestant Theology?: Traditional Religion vs. Biblical Emphasis.* Tulsa, OK: Word and Spirit Press, 2012, 110.

Scanlan, Michael and Ann Therese Shields. *And Their Eyes Were Opened: Encountering Jesus in the Sacraments.* Ann Arbor, MI; Servant Publications, 1987.

Sung, John. *The Diaries of John Sung: An Autobiography,* ed. Stephen L. Sheng. Brighton, MI: Stephen L. Sheng and Luke Sheng, 1995. Dr. John Sung was not a Pentecostal, but a holiness preacher who believed the evidence of the Baptism in the Holy Spirit "was the love of God and men," iv. He died in 1944 after 12 years of evangelistic ministry at 44 years of age.

Tappert, Theodore B., ed. *Luther: Letters of Spiritual Counsel,* Vol. 18. Library of Christian Classics Philadelphia: Westminster Press, n.d., 52.

Wallace, Daniel B. and M. James Sawyer, ed. *Who's Afraid of the Holy Spirit?*, ed. Daniel B. Wallace and M. James Sawyer. Dallas, Texas: Biblical Studies Press, 2005.

Weatherhead, Leslie. *Psychology, Religion and Healing.* New York, NY: Abingdon-Cokesbury Press. Stewart Press 2007.

OTHER BOOKS

FROM RANDY CLARK

CHANGED IN A MOMENT

DELIVERANCE

ESSENTIAL GUIDE TO HEALING

ENTERTAINING ANGELS

GOD CAN USE LITTLE OLE ME

HEALING ENERGY: WHOSE ENERGY IS IT?

HEALING UNPLUGGED

LIGHTING FIRES

POWER, HOLINESS, AND EVANGELISM

SUPERNATURAL MISSIONS

THERE IS MORE

MINISTRY MANUALS

MINISTRY TEAM TRAINING MANUAL

KINGDOM FOUNDATIONS:
A SCHOOL OF HEALING AND IMPARTATION

EMPOWERED: A SCHOOL OF HEALING AND IMPARTATION

HEALING: MEDICAL AND SPIRITUAL PERSPECTIVES

THE CORE MESSAGE SERIES

FROM RANDY CLARK

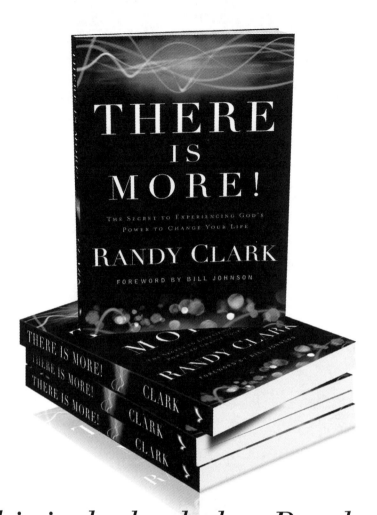

"This is the book that Randy Clark was born to write."
– Bill Johnson

In "There Is More", Randy will lay a solid biblical foudation for a theology of impartation as well as take a historical look at the impartation and visitation of the Lord in the Church. This will be combined with many personal testimonies of people who have received an impartation throughout the world and what the lasting fruit has been in their lives. You will be taken on journey throughout the world and see for yourself the lasting fruit that is taking place in the harvest field - particularly in Mozambique. This release of power is not only about phenomena of the Holy Spirit, it is about its ultimate effect on evangelism and missions. Your heart will be stirred for more as you read this book.

For this and other books go to: globalawakeningstore.com

"There is only one true Healer and His name is Jesus Christ. This book is a must read for everyone!"
- Dr. Ché Ahn, HRock Church

Healing by prayer is one thing, but whose energy it uses is another. In *Healing Energy: Whose Energy Is It?* by Randy Clark, you will understand the difference between Christian healing and the practice found in New Age, Reiki, and other present day modalities. He cuts to the core to reveal the truth about healing and it's Source. Randy Clark demonstrates how inadequate Christian views of healing have caused people to seek healing outside of biblical means. It is time for the Church to step into its destiny and to release the healing power available in Jesus. This is an excellent book that all Christian leaders must read to understand the differences between Christian healing and other cultic groups.

For this and other books go to: globalawakeningstore.com

ABOUT THE AUTHOR

Randy Clark, a noted international speaker, he is a doctoral candidate at United Theological Seminary, received his M.Div from Southern Baptist Theological Seminary, his bachelor's degree was in Religious Studies from Oakland City University. He was used of God to birth the revival that broke out in Toronto Canada in January 1994 that continued six nights a week for over twelve years. He is best known for the gift on his life for activating and imparting gifts of the Holy Spirit. The late John Wimber, was the first to recognize this grace on Randy's life. John heard the audible voice of God tell him twice that Randy would one day travel the world laying hands on pastors and leaders to activate and impart to them gifts of the Spirit. Randy also continues to demonstrate the Lord's power to heal the sick with great tenacity. While having been used to launch several famous ministers into the new level of their anointing by laying hands on them and prophesying to them, the focus of his ministry is on the average person in the congregation encouraging them that they too can be used of God in the gifts of the Spirit. His message is simple: "God wants to use you." He is the author of *There Is More* and many other books, manual/workbooks, booklets, and materials. Randy and his wife, DeAnne, reside in Mechanicsburg, PA. They have four adult children and two grandchildren.

LEARN TO MINISTER AS JESUS DID.

Do you feel a stirring in your heart to take the next step in preparation for ministry? Do you want to see healing and deliverance operating in your own life? Join us for one of our online classes in the areas of Physical Healing, Deliverance or Inner Healing. The Christian Healing Certification Program (CHCP) is a great option to expand your ministry training right from the comfort of your home.

No Prior training necessary

Courses are available to fit your schedule

Small and personal classes of 15-17 students per class

It's easy and can be done right from home

Economical and inexpensive

Join a community of online students from all over the world

For more information or to register,
visit our website at **www.healingcertification.com**
or call 717.796.9866 X124.

CHCP **Christian Healing** CERTIFICATION PROGRAM

LIFE IN THE KINGDOM IS NOT BORING

GLOBAL SCHOOL OF SUPERNATURAL MINISTRY

FROM THE FIRST TIME we encounter the King our heart's cry is answered with a resounding "yes!" We are created to take risks and dive deeply into the journey of following Christ. Come to *the Global School of Supernatural Ministry* and you will be empowered to bravely leap into the unknown, as you more intimately know the Creator.

ONSITE • ONLINE • SUMMER INTENSIVE

FOR MORE INFORMATION AND TO APPLY:

GSSM.GLOBALAWAKENING.COM OR 866-AWAKENING EXT:123

Global School of
Supernatural Ministry

Do you hunger for more?

- more power, more glory, more transformation, more of Jesus? Randy Clark has been taking teams to minster to the nations for years. Many lives, both those native to the host country and those on the international team, have been transformed by the power and presence of God. Come with us and experience the fruit for yourselves.

You can learn more and get the latest updates on all of our trips at:

imt.globalawakening.com

If you have additional questions or you would like to register for a trip, you can use the online forms or call us at:

1-866-Awakening

INTERNATIONAL
MINISTRY TRIPS

PARTNERS

RIGHT NOW, when a kingdom perspective is most needed, Randy's vision is to equip the body by lighting fires, building bridges and casting vision. It is a demanding call on his life and the expansion and explosive growth in the ministeries of Global Awakening only continues by the faithful support of those who invest their time and resources to support Randy's vision.

The vision of Global Awakening is dependent on the prayers and financial support of the Global Awakening Partners. You may not be able to go everywhere Randy goes, but you can share in the joy and heavenly reward of changed lives through the Global Awakening ministry. Whether you are on the front lines of battle or connected with the vision through your partnership, together we share the rewards and blessings.

ALL PARTNERS RECEIVE THE FOLLOWING BENEFITS:

Monthly Partner Newsletter

Monthly Prayer Theme Support

Partner Website Access

Annual Global Awakening Partner Lanyard

Preferred Conference Registration

Complimentary Services at Global Events

FIRE STARTER BENEFITS:
At least $25.00 per month or $300 annually

Benefits include:
10% off bookstore at approved Global Awakening Events, and 10% off all Global Awakening events and webcast.

BRIDGE BUILDER BENEFITS:
At least $50.00 per month or $600 annually

Additional Benefits include:
No application fee to GSSM, 25% off all Global Awakening events and webcast, plus benefits from previous tier.

GLOBAL VISION CASTER BENEFITS:
At least $100.00 per month or $1000 annually

Additional Benefits include: Early access to Voice of the Prophets and Voice of the Apostles, 50% off all Global Awakening events and webcast, plus benefits from previous tiers.

MASTER'S COMMISSION BENEFITS:
At least $500.00 per month or $5000 annually

Additional Benefits include: 25% off an international ministry trip, Global Awakening events and webcast are FREE, plus benefits from previous tiers.

PRESIDENT'S COUNCIL BENEFITS:
At least $1000.00 per month or $10,000 annually

Additional Benefits include: 50% off an international ministry trip, President's Council Personal Services, plus benefits from previous tiers.

to find out more about our partners program contact us at:

PARTNERS.GLOBALAWAKENING.COM
OR
1-866-AWAKENING.COM EXT: 121

Based in Mechanicsburg, PA, the Apostolic Network of Global Awakening is a teaching, healing and impartation ministry with a heart for the nations. Founded in 1994 by Randy Clark after his involvement with the Toronto Airport Christian Fellowship revival, the ministry exists to fulfill the biblical commissions of Jesus:

As you go preach, saying the Kingdom of heaven is at hand. Heal the sick, cleanse the lepers, raise the dead, cast out demons. Freely you have received, freely give (Matthew 10:7-8).

For a schedule of upcoming events and conferences, or to purchase other products from Global Awakening, please visit our website at: **globalawakening.com**